Brother and sister Felix and Fanny Mendelssohn enjoyed a close bond, and theirs was one of the most significant musical relationships of the nineteenth century. They shared and commented on each other's compositions, and although each was highly appreciative of the other, they also offered frank and often critical advice.

Their travels produced some of their finest music. Two of Felix's best-loved works, the *Hebrides Overture* and the *Scottish Symphony*, were inspired by his 1829 visit to Scotland, whilst Fanny's innovative piano cycle *Das Jahr* was a musical response to the tour of Italy she made in 1839–40.

Combining letters, sketches and paintings with an accompanying narrative describing their journeys, this is a unique, intimate portrait of the two Mendelssohns and the works they wrote as a result of their travels to the opposite ends of Europe.

———————

Diana Ambache has written for numerous publications, including *The Independent*, *Classical Music* magazine, *BBC Music* magazine, *Classic FM* magazine and *Musical Opinion*. As a pianist she has given concerts in more than thirty countries and has made sixteen CD recordings, many featuring the music of women composers. She was shortlisted for the prestigious European Women of Achievement in 2002 for her work pioneering the revival and promotion of music by female composers. Her book about Grazyna Bacewicz is published by Cambridge University Press (Elements *Women in Music)*.

THE SOUL
OF THE
JOURNEY

THE MENDELSSOHNS
in SCOTLAND *and* ITALY

Diana Ambache

Page ii. The Rumbling Bridge near Dunkeld.
Sketch by Felix Mendelssohn, 2 August 1829.

First published in 2021 by
Birlinn Limited
West Newington House
10 Newington Road
Edinburgh
EH9 1QS

www.birlinn.co.uk

ISBN: 978-1-78027-725-7

British Library Cataloguing-in-Publication Data
A catalogue record for this book is available
from the British Library

Typeset by Mark Blackadder

Printed and bound by Hussar Books, Poland

Contents

1

The Mendelssohns and Enlightenment Berlin

The Mendelssohn name is principally famous for the acclaimed composer Felix (1809–47). He had three siblings: Fanny (1805–47); Rebecka (1811–58), who married the mathematician Lejeune Dirichlet; and Paul (1812–74), who carried on the family business as a banker. The two eldest children were brilliant musicians. Noting Fanny's skills, Johann von Goethe wrote in a letter to Felix in 1825, 'Remember me to your equally gifted sister'.[1] Felix's reputation, however, eclipsed hers, and although her music is now being appreciated, social attitudes required her to lead the life of a *Hausfrau*. With their corresponding musical proficiency and accomplishment, it is apposite to know of their especially close rapport and mutual respect; they were the closest musical siblings of the nineteenth century.

A considerable German dynasty, the Mendelssohns were a wealthy family of the Jewish intelligentsia. Moses Mendelssohn (1729–86), Fanny and Felix's grandfather, was a philosopher of the Enlightenment, and a writer on metaphysics, politics and Hebrew heritage. His eldest son Joseph (1770–1848) founded the Mendelssohn Bank in Berlin in 1795 and became prominent among merchant bankers. The bank issued state loans for industrial development to several foreign countries, particularly Russia, and by 1815 the Mendelssohn Bank was an important part of Prussian finance. Joseph's younger brother Abraham (1776–1835), Fanny and Felix's father, joined the bank in 1804, and in the same year married Lea (1777–1842), who came from the distinguished mercantile Itzig family.

By 1800, Berlin was at the heart of European art and culture. Cosmopolitan and dynamic, forward-looking and religiously tolerant, it was the centre of royal authority and a place of vibrant social and intellectual exchange. In the eighteenth century Frederick the Great ordered the building of the St Hedwig Cathedral, and gave Berlin the State Opera (*Staatsoper*) in 1742. The Berlin University (now the Humboldt University) was founded in 1810, attracting the philosopher Hegel and the historian Leopold von Ranke, and from 1827 Berlin was the capital of Brandenburg state. While there could be a conservative cultural environment in Berlin's high society, the *Königliches Schauspielhaus* was inaugurated in June 1821 with the acclaimed premiere of Carl Maria von Weber's *Der Freischütz*, though by the late 1820s the city

Opposite. Abraham Mendelssohn (1776–1835), father of Felix and Fanny. Sketch by Wilhelm Hensel, 1829.

Lea Mendelssohn (1777–1842), mother of Felix and Fanny. Sketch by Wilhelm Hensel, 1823.

was displaying a military character, with parading soldiers.

As the Prussian capital, Berlin was naturally a key city in the Enlighten-ment; educated people pursued literary interests with the goal of emancipa-tion (from ignorance). The *Aufklärung* brought 'light' through discussions of poetry, music and philosophy. Among the middle-class Jewish women important in the Berlin salons, nurturing refined and sophisticated minds, was Abraham's older sister, Dorothy von Schlegel, a friend of Rahel Varnhagen, who hosted one of the most prominent European salons. Also notable was Fanny's namesake and aunt, Fanny von Arnstein (Lea's sister), who had been a patron of Mozart in Vienna, and whose salon was frequented by political and artistic celebrities.

Grandfather Moses was a man of distinction and a champion of Jewish emancipation. He believed in both German and Jewish culture, and gave his children a liberal education – his second son, Abraham, continued this idea of assimilation by joining the Protestant Church and having his children baptised. Moses' first son, Joseph, having founded the Mendelssohn Bank, grew the business for it to become Berlin's largest private banking house and, in 1815, it moved into the heart of the city's banking area at Jägerstrasse 51; the bank offices are now the home of the Mendelssohn Society.

Fanny Mendelssohn was born on 14 November 1805, and Felix on 3 February 1809. Both showed exceptional musical talent at an early age, and though Felix went on to a brilliant public life as a composer, pianist, organist and conductor, the cultural mores of the time meant that Fanny was constrained by nineteenth-century attitudes to a woman's social position: that of housewife and homemaker. To receive money for musical activities was not considered proper for an upper-class woman and so despite her prodigious musical talent, it was not acceptable to be a public music-maker. Michael P. Steinberg remarked, 'In their world, talent was recognised in men and women alike, but only men's lives were public.'[2] Two musical sibling prodigies are a very rare phenomenon (possibly only J. S. Bach's children, and Nannerl and Wolfgang Mozart are similarly considered). Their collaborative and symbiotic relationship suits their being considered together; a close relationship reminiscent of Helena and Hermia in *A Midsummer Night's Dream*:

> So we grew together, Like to a double cherry, seeming parted,
> But yet an union in partition; Two lovely berries moulded on one stem[3]

In the summer of 1825, Abraham purchased for the family the large house and garden at Leipziger Strasse 3, which adjoined the Tiergarten, Berlin's huge city park – previously hunting grounds, it was opened to the public by Frederick the Great in 1740. The parents guided their family with care, always looking to widen their cultural experience and knowledge; instruction was taken very seriously, with lessons beginning at 5 a.m. (only on Sundays could they sleep late, until 6 a.m.). The childrens' broad schooling encompassed many disciplines, including art, literature, philosophy, and ancient and modern languages. Their learning conformed to the ideal Classical education of sound mind and body, and Felix enjoyed physical activities, including dancing and gymnastics.

Alongside their studies, letter-writing was a carefully cultivated art in the Mendelssohn household and the tradition was maintained throughout the children's lives. Both Fanny and Felix became accomplished correspondents, with Felix's extensive writing (over seven thousand letters) making him among the more important letter-writers of that era. Even at the end of long and tiring days, they would send their story home to be shared among the family; many of their epistles were written in that knowledge.

Both for the enrichment of their children's development and for their own pleasure, the Mendelssohn parents set out to make their home a cultural and intellectual hub in the city. Centre of a large circle of friends, high-level talk in the family included discussions of Shakespeare, Friedrich Schiller, Jean Paul and Goethe; Abraham had grown up in circles where Ossian was spoken of in the same breath as Homer. The happenings and meetings at the house included music, theatrical performances and literary readings; in time they became prestigious events, being akin to an important Berlin salon. To stimulate the children's education, Abraham initiated a series of musical matinees at home, known as *Sonntagsmusiken*, in which the famous musicians of the day would come to participate. Of course, everyone was interested and benefited: Felix learnt from hearing his compositions played and Fanny used these concerts as a forum for her own performing and composing.

Starting in their apartment on Markgrafenstrasse, the Sunday performances began in 1821 and grew in importance and extent over the years. The timing was good. Berlin at that period had little else that matched the cultural value of these musical meetings, and they naturally became a magnet, attracting musicians, artists and thinkers of distinction passing through the city, who asked to be included. The broad collection of people who flocked to the house included Heinrich Heine, Adolf Lindblad, Henrik Steffens, Eduard Gans, Adolf Bernhard Marx, Franz Theodor Kugler, Johann Gustav Droysen, Alexander von Humboldt, Wilhelm Müller, Georg Wilhelm Friedrich Hegel, and other intellectual and artistic persons, famous, or to become famous later.

The family's relocation to Leipziger Strasse 3 in 1825 enabled larger congregations in the superbly spacious hall, as it had room for over two hundred people. There was a movable glass wall on the garden side, punctuated by pillars, and it could be changed into an open portico. Impressive fresco-paintings covered the walls and ceiling. The hall commanded a view of the garden, which adjoined the grounds of the Tiergarten with huge avenues of beautiful old trees.

This atmosphere of culture and education was clearly having an effect on the Mendelssohn children. A family friend, German composer and theorist Adolf Bernhard Marx, later remarked on the luck of birth: 'I soon made the acquaintance of a well-ordered and wisely led family, and learned what incalculable advantages attend one's birth into one, especially when reputation (Moses Mendelssohn!), wealth and extended connections are thrown in . . . Here I encountered someone whose every step was discussed and watched over by a father's judicious eye . . . Felix would complain to me that his father had once again become doubtful about his profession,

dissatisfied with the career of an artist, whose successes must always remain uncertain; that again and again he would suggest to him that he should become a merchant, or enter into some secure career.'[4]

Felix's friend, the actor and baritone Eduard Devrient, described how Lea encouraged Felix to be always usefully engaged: 'The mother, a highly cultivated and intelligent woman as well as an active housewife, kept the children at their work with inflexible energy. The unceasing activity of Felix, which became a necessity of life with him, is no doubt to be ascribed to early habit. If we happened to chat longer than the bread-and-butter rendered necessary, the mother's curt exclamation, "Felix, are you doing nothing?", quickly drove him away into the back room.'[5] While Devrient reported how Lea kept the children at their work with determined energy, he also commented on the importance of Abraham's influence. Both parents were keen that their children should be well-educated; guidance in all aspects of life meant that, as well as music, and the arts and culture more generally, they should also live by the best moral principles and behave respectfully – given their children's many accomplishments, the method was evidently successful. Felix later described Abraham as 'not only my father . . . but my teacher both in art and in life'.[6]

Gartenhaus at Leipzigerstrasse 3, the Mendelssohn family home, and the venue for *Sonntagsmusiken*. Wilhelm Hensel, 1851.

2

Felix

Felix Mendelssohn is now among the most popular composers of the Romantic era. The features of his Mendelssohnian style can be characterised as having ebullient melodies, balanced and colourful orchestration, elfin scherzo movements, driving rhythms and counterpoint influenced by Bach, combined with moments of intense drama and rendered with fastidious workmanship.

Clarity, great melodic richness, and adherence to the Classical tradition stand out particularly in Felix's music; he found his own personal style in his teens, which flourished as he matured, balancing graceful control with freer expressiveness. In developing an early Romantic approach to composing, he showed notable interest in extra-musical influences, such as literature and nature.

A polymath and polyglot, his astonishing versatility included being a composer who explored the contrasts of Classical and Romantic style, a virtuoso pianist and creator of fabulous improvisations, an impressive organist, able violinist and violist, an international conductor (the Gewandhaus and the Philharmonia) who was among the first to wield a baton, a teacher and founder of the Leipzig Conservatory, a music editor and scholar, a skilled artist (even his detractor Richard Wagner thought him a landscape painter of the first order) and a worldly celebrity acquainted with royalty, statesmen, scientists, artistic creatives, poets and critics. He has been described as a polite man writing polite music. Chopin thought his talents 'admirable',[1] Schumann called him 'the Mozart of the nineteenth-century' and he was 'Bach reborn', according to Liszt.

Felix was born on 3 February 1809 in Grosse Michaelisstrasse No. 14, in Hanseatic Hamburg (at that time an independent city-state). In 1811, the family escaped in disguise, as a result of the occupation by the French, and fearing their revenge for the Mendelssohn Bank's role in breaking the Napoleon Continental System blockade (an attempt to paralyse Britain through barring commercial trade). Moving to north-east Berlin, they lived on the Neue Promenade, between the River Spree and the Hackescher Markt. Born into a prominent Jewish dynasty, in the family's attempt at integration Felix was not circumcised, was given no religious education initially, and,

aged seven, on 21 March 1816, was baptised as a Protestant Christian.

Described as a child prodigy to be better than Mozart, Felix's natural musical facility showed at a very early age, both as a player and as a composer. Abraham was his guide; insightful about music, Felix said to him, 'I am often quite unable to understand how it is possible to have so accurate a judgement about music without being a technical musician, and if I could only say what I feel in the same clear and intelligent manner that you always do, I would certainly never make another confused speech as long as I live.'[2]

When Felix was six, he began taking piano lessons from his mother. In 1816, Abraham took his family to Paris, and Felix and Fanny, then seven and eleven respectively, were taught piano by Madame Bigot de Morogues. A remarkable musician, and an excellent teacher, she was married to Monsieur Bigot, Count Razumovsky's librarian, and had been a friend of Beethoven's while the Bigots lived in Vienna. Soon after their return from Paris, the Mendelssohns lived with their grandmother, in her house in the Neue Promenade, and then the children's education began more systematically. Paul Heyse was their tutor for general subjects, Ludwig Berger for the piano from 1817 to 1822, Carl Friedrich Zelter for thorough bass and composition, Carl Henning for the violin and Samuel Rösel for landscape painting. Felix learned Greek with Rebecka (two years his junior) and advanced as far as Æschylus.

Left. Felix Mendelssohn (1809–47), 1840.

Right. Felix's birthplace, Hamburg.

Showing precocious musical talent, he had memorised eight of the Beethoven symphonies by the age of eight (No. 9 was yet to be written), but his sister Fanny was also musically talented. Several well-known anecdotes illustrate that the two were intimately involved in each other's compositional projects and privy to the most particular details regarding the genesis and inspiration for their works. One of the most remarkable concerns a special task set for Felix in 1820: to write a short opera without any adult supervision. While the eleven-year-old was composing his one-act *Singspiel*, *Die Soldaten-liebschaft*,[3] only Fanny was allowed to see the score before it was rehearsed. Little wonder, then, that Fanny felt keenly the importance of her role in the budding career of her little brother, and noted in 1822: 'I have watched the progress of [Felix's] talent step by step, and may say I have contributed to his development. I have always been his only musical adviser, and he never writes down a thought before submitting it to my judgment.'[4]

Carl Zelter, leader of the Sing-Akademie in Berlin and a devotee of the music of J. S. Bach, wrote with pride to Goethe of his student on 11 March 1823: 'My Felix has entered upon his fifteenth year. He grows under my very eyes. His wonderful pianoforte playing I may consider as quite a thing apart. He might also become a great violin player . . . Imagine my joy, if we survive, to see the boy living in the fulfilment of all that his childhood gives promise of!'[5] As a teenager he wrote his Symphony No. 13 (1823), the now-famous String Octet in E flat major, Op. 20, with its airy, effervescent scherzo (1825), and the overture to *A Midsummer Night's Dream* (1826). Written as a birthday gift for his violin teacher, Eduard Rietz, the octet was completed on 15 October 1825 – the third movement is a brilliant first example of Mendelssohn's distinctive scherzo, demonstrating his inexhaustible energy, with the *leggierissimo* signalling his unique evocation of woodland fairies. As his sister Fanny later wrote, 'The whole piece is to be played staccato and pianissimo with shivering tremolos and bright flashes of trills. All is new, strange and yet so familiar and pleasing – one feels close to the world of spirits lightly carried up into the air.'[6]

Zelter wrote to Goethe on 6 November 1825: 'He takes his time by the ears and has his own way with it. He plays the piano like fury, and isn't backward at stringed instruments; and with all that he is strong and healthy, and can swim against the stream like anything. They have reviewed his Quartets and Symphonies somewhat coldly in the newspapers, but it won't hurt him. What I especially give him credit for, is the way in which he works at everything as a whole and with his whole might.'[7]

Felix, with the backing of Zelter, and with his friend the singer and actor Eduard Devrient, arranged and conducted the Bach oratorio *St Matthew Passion* in 1829. His grandmother, Bella Itzig-Salomon, had given Felix a copy of the score of the then all-but-forgotten masterpiece, and theirs was the first performance since Bach's death in 1750. Having secured soloists

Carl Friedrich Zelter, who taught Fanny and Felix thorough bass and composition.

The Sing-Akademie, Berlin, where music-lovers gathered and the Mendelssohn children studied with Carl Zelter. Eduard Gaertner, 1843.

from the Berlin Royal Opera, the performance took place at the Sing-Akademie in Berlin on 11 March 1829 and was so successful that it was repeated on Bach's birthday. Felix commented, 'To think that it should be an actor and a Jew's son that have given back to the people the greatest Christian work.'[8] The revival was a great triumph and is credited with starting the revival in Bach's music that continues to this day and that has resulted in a full-scale re-evaluation of his works.[9] The composer Hector Berlioz said, 'There is but one God – Bach – and Mendelssohn is his prophet.'[10]

As children, Fanny and Felix played a game of putting words to music; their fun may have been the root of the form developed by Felix known as *Lieder ohne Worte* ('Songs without Words'), short piano pieces that contributed enormously to his popularity. His genial charm, lyrical skill, the unassuming keyboard writing and abundant invention combined persuasively to appeal to bourgeois households of piano-enthusiasts. Even though he was highly capable with words, as his becoming one of the most important letter-writers of the nineteenth century would prove, he felt that music was a better form of communication. People usually complain that music is so ambiguous; that they are doubtful as to what they should think when they hear it, whereas everyone understands words. For me, it is just the reverse . . . single words seem to me vague, indefinite and very open to misunderstanding in comparison with real music, the music that fills one's soul with a thousand better things finer than any language.'[11]

Following Zelter's introduction to Goethe, the appreciation between Felix and the great author was mutual and reciprocal. Felix wrote to his family in November 1821: 'He is very friendly . . . One would think he was fifty years old, not seventy-three. Every morning I receive a kiss from the author of *Faust* and *Werther*, and every afternoon two kisses from Goethe, friend and father.'[12] Felix then dedicated his Piano Quartet No. 3 in B minor to Goethe. It was among his first works to be published, as his Op. 3, and was completed on 18 January 1825.

While Felix mostly carried over his father's belief that women should not publish their music, his publications did include several of Fanny's songs, issuing them under his own name. One of Fanny's contributions to his Op. 8 (published 1826–7) collection received this comment in the music periodical *Allgemeine musikalische Zeitung*: 'The last Duet [*Suleika und Hatem*] . . . appears to us to be the most beautiful of the collection. Moreover, we know the composer of these songs from his larger compositions as a man, who we believe shows great promise, whose fulfilment is not far off.'[13] Even with social attitudes discriminating against music by women, there were fluctuations in Felix's stance on Fanny's music; while returning from Scotland in 1829, he found a Broadwood piano in the saloon of the new American liner in Liverpool harbour, and he played her *Easter Sonata*. (The sonata, which depicts the Passion of Christ, was lost for 150 years, before being rediscovered in 1970. Despite being initially attributed to Felix, the manuscript was examined in 2010 and verified as being by Fanny.)

3

The Grand Tour and
Felix's Scottish Journey

There were significant creative outcomes, including music, art and writing from the two principal expeditions described here – Felix to Scotland in 1829 and Fanny to Italy in 1839–40. As a kind of educational rite of passage, the Grand Tour was a seventeenth- and eighteenth-century tradition for wealthy young men to travel Europe in search of art and Classical culture. Johann von Goethe pointed out that journeys are symbolic, with travellers tending to imagine that they are on a quest.[1] Early in his own Italian journey in 1786 he referred to it as 'an education for a lifetime',[2] and worked on learning to draw, valuing the discipline and wanting a permanent record of the magnificent scenery. Goethe wrote, 'Nothing is comparable to the new life that a reflective person experiences when contemplating a new country.'[3] A sentiment that fits with the deeply cultured interests of the Mendelssohn family.

In the early nineteenth century, English travellers went most frequently to France and Italy; but Scotland, via London, was chosen for Felix for two main reasons: the Mendelssohn family's enthusiasm for the novels of Sir Walter Scott, and the likelihood of a good travelling companion in his close friend Karl Klingemann (1798–1862), who was based in London as Secretary in the Hanoverian diplomatic corps.

Some of the rooms in the Leipziger Strasse house were rented out for use by the Hanoverian Legation, and in 1825 Karl Klingemann was among the clerks there, lodging on the top floor. He was talented, and was described as 'a diplomat, with a very refined, poetic nature'.[4] Both a skilful poet and a competent musician, he almost became one of the family. Klingemann's lifelong friendship with Felix is recorded in over three hundred letters, and much of their relationship was carried on by correspondence, beginning on 9 June 1826 and lasting until 3 October 1847, just four weeks before Mendelssohn's death. These documents show their affinity, and their constancy is demonstrated in their agreement on a so-called 'monthly letter'; however, Klingemann's laziness was well known in the Mendelssohn family, especially when he was in a depressed mood.

Ten years older than Felix, Klingemann was ahead in his career, although, with Mendelssohn's successes in various European centres, Klingemann may

Karl Klingemann (1798–1862),
Felix's friend and travelling
companion, c. 1830, by
August Grahl.

have felt outdone as their private lives later began to diverge. Even so, as his
most important advisor, Felix asked for Klingemann's guidance in 1841 about
whether to take a post at the Berlin Academy of Arts. When badgered for a
reply, Klingemann (with the now-familiar apology for lateness) recommended
acceptance. In a letter to Klingemann of April 1846, Mendelssohn wrote that
'one cannot have more than one [true friend], and I have one, and he is
Klingemann . . . It gives me the greatest joy to see your handwriting again.'[5]

Then, in September 1827, Klingemann was sent as the Legation Secretary
to London, living at 4 Hobart Place, Belgravia (where Felix later visited him),
and in 2013 English Heritage placed a Blue Plaque on the house that
Mendelssohn described as 'that smoky nest'. Klingemann wrote entertain-
ingly to the Mendelssohns about the size of London, the gloom of British
Sundays, and the difficulty of pronouncing the English *th*. At the end of their

Scottish journey, Karl and Felix together wrote a *Singspiel*, *Son and Stranger*, to honour the silver wedding anniversary of the Mendelssohn parents; it was performed in Berlin on 26 December 1829.

· · ·

Although Felix later continued on through Europe to the great Italian cities, the wilds of Scotland would be a good challenge for him. His northern journey in 1829 inspired him musically, stirring him to write two of his most cherished works: the *Hebrides Overture* and the *Scottish Symphony*. It was felt that foreign travel free of any inhibition by any other family member would both broaden his experience of life and give him confidence. Truly an educational journey, Abraham planned the *Bildungsreise*, and, when asked why he was traveling, Felix replied 'to improve myself and to make friends'.[6]

The lure of the unknown was the chief attraction of Scotland; for many Germans it was a terra incognita, or known only through the heroic Ossian, Fingal's son (in an early story from Ireland). They represented the ancient, the primitive, the grand and romantic, the wild and remote. Felix might have read the account of Scotland by the architect Karl Friedrich Schinkel in *Journal of a Visit to France and Britain 1826*, describing the view from Oban – 'the Ossianic islands and cliffs, picturesque, eerie and awesome in the confused way they are thrown together'.

Ossian was the narrator and purported author of a cycle of epic poems published in 1760 by the Scottish poet James Macpherson, who claimed to have collected word-of-mouth material in Scottish Gaelic, said to be from ancient sources, and that the work was his *translation* of that material. With their heroic ideals, the poems were influential in the course of European Romanticism, and impressed people like Thomas Jefferson and Napoleon Bonaparte. Furthermore, Ossian inspired people to compose; there was something of a flowering of musical 'Ossianism' between 1790 and 1900 – recasting into a different genre, as a kind of translation from the Ossian poems. These heroic poems and their mood of lament seem to have been a magnet in the creation of original music; composers wrote operas, cantatas and instrumental pieces. In 1780 Pietro Morandi turned *Comala* into an opera, and Harriet Wainewright's *Comála* was performed at a Haydn-Salomon concert in the Hanover Square Rooms in January 1791.

There were also some German songs associated with Ossian, including Johann Rudolf Zumsteeg's *Colma* from 1793 (translated by Goethe). Two French operas were composed in the early nineteenth century: *Ossian ou les Bardes* (1804) by Jean-François Le Sueur received seventy performances over a dozen years, and Étienne Méhul's opera *Uthal* (1806), first performed at the Opéra Comique in Paris, uses an orchestra without violins to create the dark atmosphere. It is even possible that the seven-year-old Felix could have

heard the opera by Le Sueur on his 1816 visit to Paris. The heroism of the
Ossian poems may also have been a contributory factor in motivating
Beethoven to compose the *Eroica* Symphony, Op. 55 (1804).[7] In 1814, La
Fenice, the Venice opera house, mounted *Fingallo e Comala* by Stefano Pavesi,
and two years later Schubert wrote *Ossian's song after the fall of Nathos*, D278.[8]
Gesang aus Fingal was a three-part chorus by Brahms in his Op. 17 (1860),
and in the latter part of the nineteenth century Marie Jaëll composed a
symphonic cantata in which Ossian had become a woman; *Ossiane* was based
on the poems of Jean Richepin and Victor Hugo.

Many nineteenth-century Germans saw Scotland through literary associations – as the land of Macbeth, Scott and Ossian. A visit to Scotland was
seen as the opportunity to indulge this connection with the adventurous
world of heroes, bards and warriors. The power of the romantic imagination
was such that a visit to Scotland *could* mean an encounter with Ossian, and
a reliving of Scott's novels and Burns's songs. The poems had a profound
effect on German writers, but despite Ossian's popularity in Germany, few
Germans actually made the pilgrimage to the mist-shrouded land of which
he sang, although they were infected with the Ossianic spirit and wanted to
believe in this fabled hero.

Sir Walter Scott took over from Ossian in drawing visitors to Scotland,
strengthening the Germans' ability to see the Highlands in Ossianic terms.
Sir Walter Scott has been credited with 'inventing' Scotland,[9] the Waverley
novels having been all the rage across Europe at that time. Published in 1810,
Scott's epic poem *The Lady of the Lake* lured people there, and Felix had read
it in 1820, giving him impressions of Scotland. It was hoped that Felix might
visit Abbotsford (the novelist's home, forty miles south of Edinburgh) and
meet the author, which he did on 31 July, but it was a brief encounter. Following this disappointment, Felix wrote, 'We found Sir Walter in the act of leaving
Abbotsford, stared at him like fools, drove eighty miles and lost a day for the
sake of at best one half-hour of superficial conversation.'[10]

•   •   •

Travel in the nineteenth century was of course more rudimentary than it is
now. There were borders to cross, starting with Germany's many states, and
the transport systems were less developed. Aged twenty in 1829, Felix was
not liable for military service, so it was a good time for him to go exploring,
and to show he could make his living by music. Setting off on 10 April 1829,
Abraham and Rebecka accompanied Felix to Hamburg, from where he took
a boat (the *Attwood*) to London, arriving on 21 April. Fanny's diary entry for
10 April 1829 recorded their departure: 'We got up at 4, Hensel came at 5,
and at 5:30 they [Felix, Rebecka and Abraham] departed. I remained upstairs
with Felix as long as I could, and helped him with his dressing and last-minute

Romantic Scotland: an illustration from Sir Walter Scott's *The Lady of the Lake*, which Felix read in 1820.

packing. It was cold, we watched them, as they went down the street to the East, until we could see them no longer.'[11] About to board the ship in Hamburg, Abraham wrote to Lea about Felix's elevated state of excitement: 'Felix is, as is completely correct and natural, happy and lively. He is heading off into a radiant future, but doesn't realise yet, how short life is.'[12]

The boat journey that nowadays takes a few hours took Felix several days. He had considerable interest in modern machinery, including the small paddle steamers he travelled on in Scotland, however, the passage from Hamburg was difficult, beset by storm and wind for three days; he found the turbulent crossing unpleasant and was seasick to the point of being immobile for two days. The steam packet was forced to anchor in the mouth of the Thames, in order not to collide with other ships. Weakened from seasickness and hunger, on the morning of 21 April 1829 Felix arrived at the Customs House in London, and was warmly welcomed by Klingemann as well as family friends Ignaz and Charlotte Moscheles. Ignaz, who taught Felix, wrote in 1824: 'This afternoon . . . I gave Felix Mendelssohn his first lesson, without losing sight for a moment of the fact that I was sitting next to a master, not a pupil'.[13] They became lifelong colleagues and friends, and Ignaz's son was named after Felix, who was also his godfather.

During his stay in London, Felix's first lodgings were at 103 Great Portland

Street, in Marylebone (arranged for him by Moscheles). The son of the landlord, Henry Heinke, recalled, 'Mendelssohn had two grand pianofortes in his room. He was constantly practising and often after returning home late at night would sit down to play; moreover, he used to practise on a dumb keyboard while sitting up in bed! The London street musicians disturbed him as they did Wagner. In those days there was an institution known as "The Marylebone Band", which rejoiced in the possession of a big drum. No sooner had Mendelssohn begun his morning's practice than the band would commence its lusty operations. Rushing to the top of the stairs, and putting both hands to his ears, Mendelssohn would scream out "Henry! Henry! Send them away: here is a shilling!"'

The British excursion was intended to help Felix select where he would establish his career as a musician, and to introduce him into an elite international society. For Felix, touring developed into a part of showing himself as a virtuoso, a conductor and a composer. Much bigger than Berlin, London was a desirable destination, with the British public appreciative of foreign talent. Connections there included Klingemann and Moscheles, as well as Sir George Smart, who had conducted in Berlin in October 1825. Felix's correspondence from his visit also sheds light on the public performances in London. In a letter to his father dated 1 May 1829, he wrote: 'Monday night was the Philharmonic concert. The orchestra is outstanding, full of fire and strength, and the basses and violins in particular play quite splendidly . . . The public's attention is concentrated exclusively on the instrumental pieces for the whole orchestra, so here would be the best, or rather the only good, opportunity of having my *A Midsummer Night's Dream* performed.'[14] Thus, in attending his first public concert, Felix was impressed enough with the quality of the performance to think of programming his own music for British audiences.

His first concert with the Philharmonic was on 13 May 1829. Soon after arriving in London he wrote to his family: 'London is the grandest and most complicated monster on the face of the earth . . . Things roll and whirl round me and carry me along as in a vortex.'[15] In the Argyll Rooms, on 25 May, he conducted his Symphony in C minor, Op. 11, substituting an arrangement of his octet's scherzo for the third movement. As well as having his portrait painted by the artist James Warren Childe, this visit also included his giving the British premiere of Beethoven's *Emperor* piano concerto, Op. 73. His good manners and melodious music engaged people's affection, and he became immensely popular with Philharmonic audiences.

The London monthly journal, *The Harmonicon*, reviewed Felix conducting his first symphony in July 1829: 'The author conducted it in person, and it was received with acclamations. The audience wished the *Adagio* to be repeated, but M. Mendelssohn did not construe the continued applause as an encore. The Scherzo and Trio, however, were instantly called for a second

Felix Mendelssohn on his first visit to London, by J. W. Childe, 1829.

time, and the band seemed most happy to comply with the demand. He was surprised at such accuracy of performance, and expressed his satisfaction in terms that were highly gratifying to this most excellent band.'[16]

Felix's versatility across the arts was impressive; he has been called a Renaissance man. As well as his notable musical talents, he was a linguist (reading novels in English, Italian and Spanish), a habitual letter-writer and a skilful artist. In December 1828, Wilhelm Hensel (1794–1861), his future brother-in-law, gave him a small pocket notebook, which he always kept with him and used as a kind of diary, and in which he drew many of the engaging scenes that he saw, including some thirty sketches made in Scotland, along with notes of the journey. His Highland sketches are now held in albums in the Bodleian Library and the Yale Beinecke Collection, ranging from brief scribbles to fully completed paintings, recognisable as well-known landmarks.

While Britain was a little further along than Germany in the Industrial Revolution, transport was still rudimentary. The recent extension of steamer trips sometimes allowed the two friends to break out of the confines of conventional guidebook advice. Felix's journey to Scotland was made between 22 and 24 July, by stagecoach. Anticipating their journey, Klingemann wrote, 'I never see these stages [coaches] without pleasure. The big carriages, on which the passengers cling like wasps on a sweet pear, roll so swiftly and merrily along that my heart rejoices at the thought of next spring, when the stage, with its team of four strong horses, is to convey me eighty miles a day along the smooth roads and across the green, hilly country, full of towns, villages and cottages, to Scotland.'[17] Travelling via York and Durham, the first part of the friends' drive of a little under a hundred miles north to Stamford (Lincolnshire) would have taken them something like twenty hours, and, by 1830, cost £1.30.[18]

Felix wrote home on 28 July 1829: 'It is Sunday as we arrive in Edinburgh. We then proceed across The Meadows to two devilishly steep rocks, which are called Arthur's Seat and scramble up them . . . All around, the city spreads out before you, and in the middle of it there is a castle perched like a bird's nest on a cliff, beyond the castle are more meadows, then hills, and a wide

The Edinburgh skyline from Arthur's Seat. Sketch by Felix Mendelssohn, 28 July 1829.

river, across the river more hills, then a more imposing mountain where Stirling Castle appears, and this is already way off in the distance; behind it there is a pale shadow they call Ben Lomond . . . How can I describe it? When God takes up panorama painting you can expect something terrific . . . Tomorrow the Highlanders are having a *bagpipe* competition . . . I was just as pleased when I went for a swim in the sea today, paddling about alone in the open water for a few minutes; I was well submerged in the Scottish sea, which tastes very salty – Doberan is lemonade by comparison.'[19]

Felix must have had a fine day for climbing Arthur's Seat in Edinburgh and he was overwhelmed by the beauty: 'Few of my Switzerland reminiscences can compare to this.'[20] He stayed in Edinburgh at 19 Albany Street at the home of his host George Hogarth, the lawyer, cellist, composer and (later) music critic for monthly journal *The Harmonicon*. Felix also dined with Finlay Dun, a fellow composer, who lived at Number 33. A letter of 31 August 1829 from his sister Fanny refers to a performance of Felix's String Quartet in E flat major (Op. 12) at the Hogarths', and it was probably Hogarth, George Thomson (Hogarth's father-in-law) and Dun who performed this with Felix. While staying in Edinburgh, Finlay Dun and Hogarth took the composer to a bagpipe competition, as mentioned by Felix (above) and recorded by Dun: 'I had the happiness to be his companion at the Competition of Pipers, and on some other occasions when he heard Scottish music, and it was with pride and pleasure that I observed the interest he took in the melodies of my country. [Mendelssohn] listened most attentively to every piece, drawing comparisons between the powers of different performers and their instruments, and he afterwards spoke warmly of the spirit-stirring character of the warlike strains of the North.'[21]

Mendelssohn later expressed antipathy towards 'national music'. A letter from Llangollen dated 25 August 1829 shows his reaction: 'Anything but national music! May ten thousand devils take all folklore. Here I am in Wales, and oh how lovely, a harpist sits in the lobby of every Inn of repute playing so-called folk melodies at you – i.e. dreadful, vulgar, fake stuff, and *simultaneously* a hurdy-gurdy is tootling out melodies, it's enough to drive one crazy, it's even given me a toothache.'[22]

On 30 July, Hogarth took Felix to see Holyrood Palace, the inspiration for his *Scottish Symphony*, which was described in a letter home: 'In the evening twilight we went today to the palace where Queen Mary lived and loved . . . Everything around is broken and mouldering, and the bright sky shines in. I believe I found today in that old chapel the beginning of my Scotch symphony.'[23] In the ruined chapel Mendelssohn noted down the opening bars of the symphony that would take him thirteen years to complete, and which also has echoes of the pipe music he heard with Hogarth. Felix clearly enjoyed his visit: 'How kind the people are in Edinburgh, and how generous is the good God! The Scotch ladies also deserve notice.'[24] While this appears to be the strongest source for his *Scottish Symphony*, there is perhaps another connection: dated 4 September 1829, 'Coed-du', the first of his *Three Fantasies*, Op. 16, bears notable resemblance to the introduction to the *Scottish Symphony*, in key (A minor), tempo (*Andante con moto*) and melody. These three pieces were written for the three daughters of John Taylor, while staying with them near Holywell, in Flintshire, North Wales, on his return journey to London.

Thanks to his sketches and notes, it's possible to describe Felix's Scottish journey in detail. 26–30 July: to Edinburgh. 31 July: to Abbotsford. 1–3 August: started out on a steamer from Newhaven harbour up the Firth of Forth to Stirling, and from Stirling in an open carriage to Perth. The next day (Sunday 2nd) Felix walked the twenty-one miles to Dunkeld and visited the famous waterfalls on the River Braan, and then walked a further twenty-one miles on the Monday to Blair Atholl. He would certainly have visited Ossian's Cave, near the river, and the Hermitage (now National Trust for Scotland). According to legend, Ossian died in a cave, and this was probably Felix's first Scottish encounter with Ossianic lore.

Between 4 and 6 August they visited the Bruar Falls, the Pass of Killie-crankie, Tummel Bridge ('lonely, deluged in rain, with people speaking unintelligible Gaelic'[25]), the Falls of Moness and the single street of Fort William. They even bought a horse and cart to make better progress along Loch Tay to Crianlarich. Thanks to General Wade's military road, they covered fifty miles in spite of the weather; Klingemann wrote of 'thick

Map showing Felix and Karl's journey round Scotland, July–August 1829.

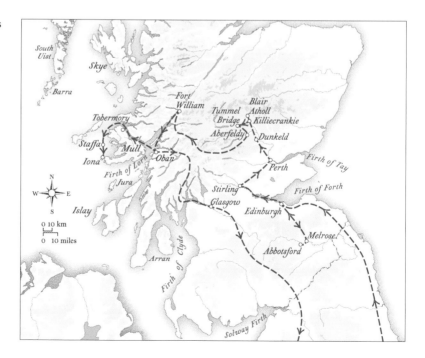

drizzling rain . . . the mighty mountains were up to their knees in clouds and looked out again from the top.'[26] They reached Fort William on 6 August in time to take the weekly steamer down to Oban on 7 August; the *Maid of Morven* left Glasgow every Thursday for Inverness. They were once again among people, enjoying sunshine and sea-green colours.

Klingemann's letter of 7 August 1829 described 'The youngsters of Tobermory, the capital of the Isle of Mull, are merrily bustling by the Harbour; the Atlantic Ocean, which appears to contain abundance of water, is quietly riding at anchor, the same as our steamer . . . By the harbour of Oban Bruce's Rock rises up, where he is said to have done some great deed or other . . . the relic [Bruce's brooch] was stolen, and at last found in possession of a lady-descendent of Rob Roy.'[27]

The elements were a major aspect of this journey and later Felix wrote from Llangollen in Wales (25 August 1829), 'The summer is gone, and without having sent a single summer day. Yesterday was a *good* day, i.e., I only got

The Pass of Killiecrankie, sketch by Felix Mendelssohn, 3 August 1829.

Dunollie Castle near Oban, view towards the Hebrides. Sketch by Felix Mendelssohn, 7 August 1829.

soaked three times, kept my cloak over my shoulders the whole day, and saw the sun a few times through the clouds. *Bad* days are beyond imagination; a raging, whistling storm has been blowing for four weeks almost without interruption . . .'[28]

Steam was the very newest piece of transport; the world's first steamboat had been built in Glasgow in 1805, and nearly twenty years later they were enabling people to enjoy the marvellous scenery of the Western Isles; there were many, the two friends noticed, in Glasgow Harbour. August was the first month that this transport was advertised, and Felix and Klingemann didn't want to miss the once-a-week steamer. With Felix again suffering from seasickness, on 7 August they took the *Maid of Morven* down Loch Linnhe to Oban. The next morning the *Ben Lomond* took passengers around the top of Mull, to Tobermory (then Mull's only harbour), a community of about a hundred houses. Out in the Atlantic nearly everyone was nauseous, apart from Klingemann. Felix's discomfort meant he left no record, but it was on

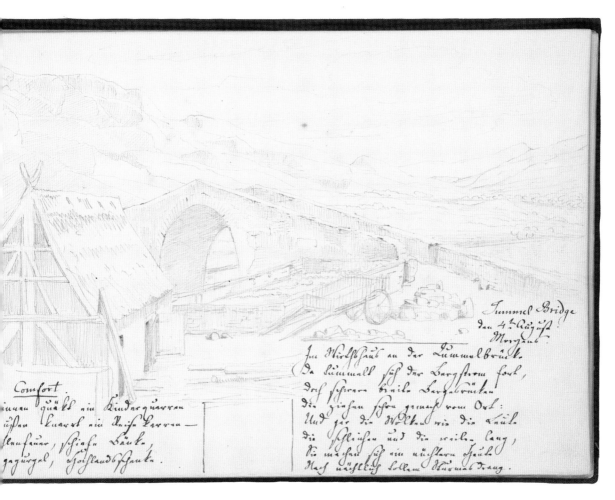

Tummel Bridge, near Pitlochry. Sketch by Felix Mendelssohn, 4 August 1829.

Saturday, 8 August 1829, that they made their memorable trip to Staffa and Fingal's Cave.

Staffa's exceptional geological features are recognised as having great importance, and the whole island's ecosystem is now a Site of Special Scientific Interest, thanks to its rocks, soil, climate, topography and the influences of its marine location. Fingal's Cave was formed entirely from hexagonal, joined basalt columns, in a lava flow some sixty million years ago (similar in structure to the Giant's Causeway in Northern Ireland). The columns were formed from a single, massive stream of ash, which gradually cooled and solidified. As the material settled, its volume shrank slightly, creating the narrow spaces which separate the columns. Theoretically, if the cooling process had occurred uniformly, every column should be perfectly hexagonal; but there were a multitude of minor variations in the rock itself, from its pattern of losing temperature, which led to the considerable diversity in the size and form of the columns. Keats described it in a letter to his father: 'Suppose now the

Giants who rebelled against Jove had taken a whole mass of black columns and bound them together like bunches of matches, and then, with immense axes, had made a cavern in the body of these columns. Of course the roof and floor must be composed of the broken ends of the columns. Such is Fingal's Cave, except that the sea has done the work of excavation, and is continually dashing there.'[29]

In 1772, Sir Joseph Banks had recognised that Staffa's coarse basalt resembled the Giant's Causeway in Ireland, and a French geologist excited by Ossian, Faujas de Saint-Fond, was marooned on the island for several days in 1784. In 1800, Sarah Murray, a fifty-six-year-old from Kensington, rowed herself into Fingal's Cave to be told she was only the ninth woman to reach Staffa, and in 1803 Dorothy and William Wordsworth visited.

Fingal's Cave (and Staffa) is the most famous and best documented of the Ossian-associated sights, being a perfect setting for heroic exploits of old, as well as an ancient earthly wonder. There were real mists, the drenching mists of the Scottish Isles; and metaphorical mists, the hazy mists of time – a foggy cloud atmosphere captured by Felix in his *Overture*'s introduction. By the mid-1820s there was sufficient tourist trade for oarsmen to be hired to ferry them from Mull, weather permitting, and in 1826 people sailed there by steamer. A mild irony was that the only time people were able to get to Staffa was when the weather was un-Ossianic. Fingal himself seemed to retreat to the back of people's minds when they saw the marvels of the cave itself.

Klingemann nearly persuaded Felix to forego the pilgrimage to the cave in order to avoid his inevitable seasickness. So, while Klingemann was in a fit state to recount the journey, four days later, Felix only wrote: 'What's in between was most horrible; travel, seasickness, people, places. Klingemann has described everything, and you will accept my apologies if I take a brief rest. The best I have to report stands in the music above [the manuscript of the opening bars of the *Overture*].'[30]

The description of the island by Klingemann is light-hearted and entertaining, though there is small mention of Staffa and more about their fellow passengers: 'Staffa with its strange, basalt pillars and caverns, is in all picture books. We were put out in boats and lifted by the hissing sea up the pillar stumps to the celebrated Fingal's Cave. A greener roar of waves surely never rushed into a stranger cave – its many pillars making it look like the inside of an immense organ, black and resounding, and absolutely without purpose, quite alone, the wide grey sea within and without.'[31] Klingemann's letter home on 10 August 1829 is evocatively romantic compared with Felix's brief statement of the unpleasantness of getting to Staffa. Although they got there, and Felix was in no state to appreciate its wonders, he was engaged by its natural beauty and rich history of fact and fable that drew from him a distinct skill – a musical description of landscape. Fingal's Cave was also known as *Am Uamh Binn* (the Cave of Melody), and Felix's response shows him as a

consummate painter of musical-tone, the literary, pictorial and musical elements of his imagination merging productively.

Klingemann's attitude was that so long as Felix and he were enjoying a light-hearted holiday, they could take time to admire the scenery and sights. However, whilst enamoured with the idea of Scotland, they were also aware of its harsh reality. The Hebrides and Scotland were far from being simply the homes of romantic bards and heroes, and the setting for their legendary exploits. Instead, while Felix and Karl knew of the 1689 Jacobite victory at the Battle of Killiecrankie, they were also aware of the Highland Clearances; poverty was visible and the primitive conditions in the inns underlined this.

Returning southward, between 9 and 15 August, Felix and Klingemann went via Loch Fyne and Inverary to Glasgow, and on to Loch Lomond and the Trossachs. The lack of public transport meant that they sometimes walked about twenty miles in a day. While Klingemann was thirty, Felix was twenty; the whole journey was another major achievement for this cultured young man.

Fingal's Cave, Staffa. Aquatint by William Daniell (1769–1837). The theme for *The Hebrides Overture* actually occurred to Mendelssohn the evening before setting sail for Staffa.

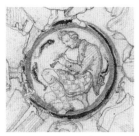

Das Rad (The Wheel), by
Wilhelm Hensel, August 1829.
Felix, in a kilt, is shown as the
hub.

In August 1829, Wilhelm Hensel sketched *Das Rad* (the wheel), with family
and friends as spokes, and Felix as the hub in a kilt – the allusion seems to
illustrate the idea that Scotland was very much in their minds.

Fanny's letter to Felix of 15 August 1829 discusses this portrayal of their
close social group: 'What is a wheel? . . . a gay get-together in Charlottenburg,
on Midsummer's Day . . . a pictorial representation had been sketched on
that day in free outline . . . Don't you know the youth in the middle, the hub
of the wheel, in English jacket and Scottish accessories? . . . the entire fine
company revolves around him and dances to his piping . . . a curious dolphin
munches on the freshly-written music in his pocket . . . The C over her head
containing the moon with the man in it will disclose what you don't know
yet.[32] The dainty figure next to her dances a gallop with your shadow since
you're not on hand . . .'[33]

4
The *Hebrides Overture*

Felix Mendelssohn was the first to use the term 'concert overture'. Based on the overtures to romantic operas, these one-movement works took either the classical sonata form or the free form of a symphonic poem, and in Felix's *Hebrides Overture* the programme doesn't interfere with his strong sense of form. From his Scottish tour, Felix was inspired to compose the overture *The Hebrides* (Fingal's Cave) in 1829–30. It's possible that his view of the setting in the Hebrides was coloured by reading James Macpherson's fabricated translation of poems by Ossian, but more likely his own visit to the mysterious cave on Staffa and the idea of the wash of the waves was the source of his creativity. However, one of music history's fictions is that the *Hebrides* theme was evoked by the sight of Fingal's Cave itself. In reality, some years after his visit, Felix told his friend Ferdinand Hiller that while the cave was the inspiration for the theme, it had actually occurred to him the evening *before* setting sail for Staffa. In a note to Fanny, Felix jotted down the opening of the *Overture*: 'In order to make you understand how extraordinarily the Hebrides affected me, the following came into my mind there'.[1]

In fact, Felix only saw the cave on 8 August. So, it is more likely that he was prompted by the sight of the whole misty scene and crashing waves, as well as one of the lonely isles that he saw from the crossing from Oban to Tobermory. Indeed, the first version of the *Overture* was entitled *Der einsame Insel* ('The Lonely Isle'), suggesting he could have been excited by the many islands they had seen while travelling to Tobermory. Whatever the title, the natural imagery is powerful, his memories of the desolate, rugged Highland terrain matched by the physical remoteness of the Hebridean islands. Moreover, storm-tossed seas were an important subject in Romantic poetry, symbolising the distressed individual battling the forces of nature.

The *Overture* was later worked on in the incongruous atmosphere of Venice and Rome, with Felix noting 'what a strange production it is'. In a letter to Fanny of 21 January 1832 he wrote, 'I do not consider it finished. The middle movement forte in D major is very stupid, and the whole modulations savour more of counterpoint than of train oil and seagulls and salt fish, and it ought to be exactly the reverse.'[2] It was premiered on 14 May 1832 at a Philharmonic concert in London, conducted by Mozart's pupil Thomas

Attwood, and Breitkopf und Härtel published it in 1834. Attwood was an early friend of Felix's in London, and serendipitously he had arrived on the boat called *Attwood*. Moscheles recorded that 'no one seemed to understand' the *Overture*; however, music critic and opera manager William Ayton thought Felix 'one of the most original geniuses of the age'.[3]

The development of the *Overture* can be seen in Felix's personal correspondence. Writing from Wales in September 1829 he refers to a new composition as *Hebridengeschichte* ('Hebrides Tale'). A letter from Vienna a year later states, 'During my next leisure time I will have the *Hebrides Overture* finished'.[4] Even though he travelled through Graz, Vienna, Venice and Rome in the next few months, his musical thoughts returned to the rocky, uninhabited outcrop off the west coast of Scotland. *Die Hebriden* (No. 5) went through further revisions, and was played by Felix on the piano for Hector Berlioz in Rome in 1831. Berlioz wrote to Ferdinand Hiller on 1 January 1832, 'It was in Rome that I had my first experience of that delicate, pretty, richly coloured substance known as the Fingal's Cave Overture. Mendelssohn had just completed it and gave me a fairly accurate idea of the piece, such was his prodigious ability to play the most complicated scores on the piano.'[5]

Animated by a different source, and from its depiction of a mood, the *Hebrides Overture*, Op. 26, is an early example of a musical tone-poem, a single-movement piece written to evoke a mood or story. It was completed on 16 December 1830, revised and renamed *Overture to the Isles of Fingal* and dedicated to King Frederick William IV of Prussia (the cousin of Prince Albert). As well as being called a concert overture, and tone-painting a Scottish landscape or seascape, the representation led musicologist Edward Lockspeiser to declare the work one of the first instances of musical impressionism.[6]

In 1844, Felix conducted some of the London Philharmonic Society concerts, and '. . . this overture (in manuscript) was tried at a morning trial performance, when, it would appear, it did not "go" to the composer's satisfaction, but Mr Anderson, the Hon Treasurer, who expressed his admiration of the fine work, was surprised to hear Mendelssohn say, with some heat, that he was so much displeased with it that he should burn it, and that, certainly, it should never be heard in public. Mr Anderson then said: "You have often expressed your admiration of my good master, Prince Albert; I am sure it would gratify him to hear a new work of yours, so pray let me give him that pleasure by means of the Queen's private band." Mendelssohn agreed, on condition that the *Overture* should never be publicly performed, and gave Mr Anderson the original orchestral parts. The *Overture* was often played at Buckingham Palace and Windsor Castle, to the admiration of Her Majesty and the Prince. Some time after the composer's lamented death, Mr Anderson wrote to Cécile, Mendelssohn's widow, informing her of all that had passed with respect to this overture, and requested permission to perform it at Mrs Anderson's next benefit concert. The permission was kindly given in 1849, and shortly after this first performance, it was played by the Philharmonic Orchestra, and has become, since then, a stock work.'[7]

As so often with Felix, he constantly felt the need to make improvements and adjustments, as expressed in his letter from London on 11 May 1832: 'I have significantly changed and improved the *Hebrides*; it will be rehearsed for the first time at the Philharmonic tomorrow morning'.[8] Felix termed his severe self-critical faculty his 'revision devil'.[9] The *Overture*'s first version had been finished at the end of 1830, and the name had changed to *The Hebrides*. He continued to revise the *Overture*, with notable changes between the London performances in the summer of 1832 and eventually conducting the Berlin premiere in January 1833. Felix created a blustery work, evoking the mysterious atmosphere of the cave, and the surge and power of the sea. The first audience was resistant to the charms of a brooding Scottish seascape and reviews criticised it for being 'too serious for the concert public'. This was the cue for more changes, and in 1835 the score was published in Berlin as *Die Fingals-Höhle*.

A letter to Fanny suggests that he wrote the *Overture* to represent his experiences in the Hebrides: the dramatic sound-world of the cave is conjured up in the opening by violas, cellos and bassoons. Built on a short, haunting phrase, the formal treatment is skilfully handled, varied with light and shade. Possibly reflecting the bleak beauty of the islands, and certainly emulating watery movement, within the opening six bars the music shifts starkly from B minor to D major to F sharp minor. Much of the music, and notably the second theme, evokes rolling waves and the wash of the sea.

While being based on the basaltic formations of Staffa, with its mythical associations, Felix's musical vision includes references to human conflict. Near the end of the exposition there are wind fanfares, with stark repetition by trumpets and horns creating a military atmosphere. After the reprise, the fanfares return, softly subdued, with a rare self-quotation of a humorous bit of musical autobiography, lifted from a passage of his *Liederspiel* (written for his parents' 1829 Silver Anniversary), *Die Heimkehr aus der Fremde*. Another personal reference is his reuse of a turbulent unison passage from his last string symphony (the unnumbered *Sinfoniesatz* in C minor); the C minor/three flats of 1823 are turned into B minor/two sharps in the overture of 1830 – both have a conspicuous turn to the Neapolitan (the lowered second degree of the scale).

Although constructed within conventional sonata form, the music gives the impression of being free-flowing; Felix had a natural skill in shaping form to his musical expression. The review in the *Harmonicon* said, 'So far as music is capable of imitating, the composer has succeeded in his design; the images impressed on his mind he certainly excited, in a general way, in ours: we may even have heard the sounds of the howling of the wind and roaring of the

Overleaf. Letter by Felix Mendelssohn to the family, 7 August 1829, with his sketch for the opening of the *Hebrides Overture*.

Auf einer Hebride. d. 7ten August 1829. Um zu verdeutlichen, wie seltsam mir ...

[musical notation]

Violini. — Viola — Violoncelle — Allegro moderato C Dur — C.B. — Sempre piano.

Glasgow d. 11 Aug. Und liegt da Allerlei dazwischen. Die gräßlichsten Sachen möglich giebt es nicht, wie ich. Heut schicken nach London gehabt
von harten Lostrennungen seit heut Abend geplagt, die mir jetzt
jetzt Mißbrauch ist, d. wie noch in ihrer Verschwendung. Heut zu-
gegangen sachen, d. ihr merkt mich nachsichtigen, wenn ich mich
wenden habe genau in den obigen Musiktakten, da beschreib
ich euch genau. Verzeiht also diesmal. Ich zeichne sehr fleißig,
Sächelchen besser gelungen sind als früher. Auch geht mir der Loch
gebraucht. Morgen gehn wir nach Lomond u. den Ben, nach der
Woche sind wir wieder hier, d. von da aus kehren wir zu-
Mit Herrmann und den, Klingers, geht nach London zu-
welchen können. In Heppen denk ich noch 3 Wochen
Continent zu gehn. Schickt doch, es möglich, ruhige Zeit
Euch d. lebt wir wohl.

Trombe / Corni / sempre piano / senza Violini: / pp

waves . . . Nothing living is seen, except the seabird, whose reign is there undisturbed by human intruder.'[10]

As a musical form, overtures had previously been written as an introduction to an opera, but in the early nineteenth century Weber wrote some works intended to be separate items for the concert hall and, in 1821, the twelve-year-old Felix attended the premiere of Weber's opera *Der Freischütz*, and had been swept away by what Zelter described as 'nonsense and gunpowder'.[11] Felix's *A Midsummer Night's Dream* (1826) has been designated the first concert overture, and more followed, including the *Hebrides*. In the years since, people have found other uses for that piece of music, most notably in Slavko Vorkapich and John Hoffman's 1941 experimental film *Moods of the Sea*, and in Luis Buñuel's 1930 film *L'Âge d'Or*. Furthermore, the Warner Brothers *Inki* cartoons featured a minimalist and expressionless mynah bird who, accompanied by the *Fingal's Cave* music, utterly disregards any obstacles or dangers. Even more bizarrely it can be heard in an a cappella arrangement in the video game Crash Twinsanity.

· · ·

Between writing the *Overture* and the *Scottish Symphony*, Felix met Cécile Jeanrenaud (1817–53) in 1836. She was the daughter of the former minister at the Calvinist Luther Church in Frankfurt am Main, where Abraham and Lea had been baptised on 4 October 1822; her mother, Elizabeth Souchay, was a visual artist. In the spring of 1836 Johann Nepomuk Schelble was due to conduct Felix's new oratorio, *St Paul*, Op. 36, but was ill and the premiere was postponed. Instead, the twenty-seven-year-old Felix took to the podium to conduct the singers in another performance on 22 May 1836 at the Düsseldorf Festival. Among the sopranos was a teenage girl who caught Felix's eye. He later wrote to his closest friend about her 'luxurious golden-brown hair' and her 'most bewitching deep blue eyes'.[12] They married on 28 March 1837 in Frankfurt, when he was twenty-eight and she twenty, and they went on to have five children.

Abraham had once said to friend and singer Eduard Devrient, 'I am afraid that Felix's censoriousness will prevent his getting a wife'.[13] Apparently not. Devrient described the effect Cécile had on Felix: 'In Cécile Jeanrenaud he was to find the young woman who was to complete and calm his existence . . . Felix showed in his dawning affection his characteristic conscientiousness. He tore himself away, and travelled down the Rhine, in order to test his passion far away from the magic circle of the beloved maiden, but he found his heart so deeply implicated, that he could return with a good conscience in the middle of September and betroth himself. Cécile was one of those sweet, womanly natures, whose gentle simplicity, whose mere presence, soothed and pleased . . . Shakespeare's words "My gracious silence" applied to her no less than the wife of Coriolanus.'[14]

Opposite. Cécile Jeanrenaud (1817–1853) at the time of her engagement to Felix. Oil painting by Eduard Magnus, 1836.

5
The *Scottish Symphony*

Also inspired by Felix's Scottish journey, the Symphony No. 3 in A minor, Op. 56, was written and revised between 1829 and 1842. Although designated No. 3, the *Scottish Symphony* was the last of Felix's five symphonies, eventually completed thirteen years after his trip.

Even before their tour, Felix indicated that he would write a symphony based on his Scottish experiences; his letter from Rome of 22 November 1830 to his sisters talks of preparing to perform Handel's *Solomon*: '. . . After this work I am thinking of composing the Christmas music *Vom Himmel hoch* and the A minor symphony.'[1] Felix created two symphonic romantic landscapes, giving impressions of the north and the south. He wrote the *Italian Symphony*, Op. 90, in 1830–1; it was premiered in Berlin on 13 May 1833. This symphony (No. 4) was inspired by the sunny vibrant colours and atmosphere of Italy, and contrasts tellingly with the more sombre presence of the north in No. 3. Felix dated it 20 January 1842, and he played it through to the composer William Sterndale Bennett, who arrived in Berlin the following day. In 1979, the German musicologist Ludwig Finscher labelled it a 'Walter Scott Symphony', suggesting influence from Scott's poetry and novels.[2] The English premiere was at the Philharmonic on 13 June 1842, with Haydn's Clock Symphony (No. 101), and two piano fantasias performed by Sigismond Thalberg; composer and musicologist G. A. Macfarren thought the symphony had overwhelming pathos: 'that deep, intense, and soulful feeling which dives down into the bottom of the human heart'.[3]

The opening of the *Scottish Symphony* came to Felix after visiting Holyrood Palace. His letter to his family (Friday, 31 July 1829, quoted above on page 19) described his inspiration. Scottish history in general, and a preoccupation with Mary, Queen of Scots in particular, are key elements in appreciating the *Scottish Symphony*. Felix is likely to have known Friedrich Schiller's *Maria Stuart* (1800), which deals with the final days of the queen's life before her execution. The dark colour of the music's funereal opening suggests that she was in Felix's thoughts as he composed; further references are detectable in the melancholy march-like tread of the slow movement, and in the coda to the finale. The battle sequences in the finale call to mind the battles of which Mendelssohn and Klingemann would have been aware:

Opposite. The *Scottish Symphony*: the composer's autograph score.

35

the Battle of Killiecrankie in 1689 (subject of a poem by Klingemann) and the 1745 Jacobite uprising in particular. And no doubt passing through Glencoe must have reminded the travellers of the massacre that took place there three years after Killiecrankie.

The *Scotch Symphony* (as Felix called it) proved hard to finish, as he described in a letter from Rome on 29 March 1831: 'Spring is in all her bloom, there is a genial blue sky outside, and my coming journey to Naples is ever in my mind. So, it's not surprising that I find it impossible to return to my misty Scottish mood. I have therefore laid aside my Scotch Symphony for the time being.'[4] It was nearly thirteen years after the initial inspiration in Holyrood Chapel that he conducted the first performance in Leipzig on 3 March 1842.

The lengthy gestation period began during the week-long stay in Edinburgh, starting in July 1829, during which Felix climbed Arthur's Seat, and sketched the familiar view of Edinburgh Castle and the Royal Mile. He worked on the symphony in 1830–1, but then put it aside for some years. Fanny had been encouraging Felix to find a wife, and in 1836 he met Cécile Jeanrenaud, marrying her the following March. The symphony was finally completed in January 1842, and premiered at the Leipzig Gewandhaus in March that year. Felix also conducted it in London on 13 June, and then went to Buckingham Palace on 9 July to ask Queen Victoria if he might dedicate it to her. He later wrote from Frankfurt describing his visit to Buckingham Palace, and the (now well-known) singing of Queen Victoria; both the queen and Prince Albert were accomplished singers and pianists. Felix asked her permission to dedicate the A minor symphony to her, since that was the ostensible reason for this visit to England, and because the English name would suit the Scottish piece so well. It was published in 1843, with a dedication to the queen.

With its romantic genesis, the symphony suggests the atmosphere of Scottish legend. It is a work inspired by the impression of Scotland, rather than storytelling; the pictures from the music are more like a series of images. There are stern, martial fanfares, which interrupt the flow of the dirge-like adagio, and hints of tribal warfare in the contrapuntal strife of the finale (entitled *Allegro guerriero*). Other Scottish influences can be detected in some of the melodic material, such as in the bubbling scherzo (in two/four time, rather than the usual three/four); it has the energy of a native Scottish dance, perhaps imitating folk music.

Responding to scenes of his travels, and incorporating this idea of reminiscence, Felix was part of the developments occurring in orchestral music during the early nineteenth century. Formally, the symphony is Felix's most ambitious attempt at an integrated symphonic structure; this was sufficiently unusual for the published score to carry a warning against the customary long pauses between movements – he specified *attacca* (no pauses). The four

movements are played without a break,[5] which stresses the thematic integrity of the work, and each following movement seems to take up from the previous one's ending.

The scoring of the opening is unusual – for woodwind and violas, with no upper strings until bar seventeen. It seems that perhaps Mary, Queen of Scots was in his thoughts during this slow introduction, which sets the scene in the 'broken and mouldering' chapel. The minor mode and subdued mood continue in the *Allegro un poco agitato*: violins and clarinet play the long main theme *pianissimo*. Indeed, the sombreness even extends to the plaintive second subject, in E minor. Eventually the full force of the full orchestra arrives, and is particularly effective in the storm sequence in the recapitulation.

Without a break, the music continues on to the scherzo, marked *Vivace non troppo*; with Felix's characteristic effervescent energy, it is certainly outdoor music and possibly describes a gathering of merry-making Highlanders. The

Prince Albert playing a Bach chorale on the organ at Buckingham Palace, to Queen Victoria and Felix, 1842.

The concert hall at the old Gewandhaus, Leipzig, where Felix became musical director in 1835.

music is based on the remarkably consonant pentatonic scale (as used by the bagpipes). The beautiful *Adagio* has been called a lament for Mary, Queen of Scots, whereas the fast and warlike finale, *Allegro guerriero*, depicts both a battle and the wildness of the Scottish moors; soldiers on a quick march are suggested by the four-square tread of the lower instruments, and restless syncopations and wild fugal passages evoke the chaos of fighting. The curious coda seems to have Mary in mind again, and refers to Felix's *Ave Maria*, Op. 23 No. 2, which has the same notes, key and time signature.

The following was included in Charles Gounod's memoir of May 1843: 'I left for Leipzig. This was where Mendelssohn was living and his sister Madame Hensel had given me a letter of introduction to him. My reception at his hands was wonderful – I use this word deliberately to describe the condescension with which a man of his standing welcomed a lad who must have seemed to him to be no more than a schoolboy . . . Mendelssohn was the Director of the Gewandhaus Orchestra. Although the orchestra was not meeting at that time of year, the concert season being over, he was kind and thoughtful enough to bring it together for me and allowed me to hear his fine Scottish Symphony in A minor. He made me a present of the score and wrote a few friendly words on it.'[6] This elegant and sympathetic manner of Felix's was noticed by other musical contemporaries, and it brought him great respect.

Despite the weather and poverty, misty, wet Scotland made a big impression on Felix; the violent history and the natural world animated his creativity, so he expressed himself in music and art. Influences and future developments continued, not least in the world of oratorio and Felix's support of William Sterndale Bennett. In a letter home from Glasgow on 15 August 1829, Felix wrote: 'We had weather to make trees and rocks crash. We wandered for ten days without meeting a single other traveller. Villages turned out to be just a few huts huddled together. Whisky is the only drink. It's no wonder the Highlands have been called melancholy. But we two have been happy enough, laughing, rhyming, sketching, growling at each other and at the world . . . eating everything edible and sleeping for twelve hours every night . . . We won't forget it as long as we live.'[7]

On his return to London from his tour of Scotland and Wales, Felix met with an accident – on 17 September he was thrown out of a carriage and his leg was severely hurt. The injury kept him in London for two months; he had been planning to be back in Berlin for Fanny's wedding, and had begun writing an organ piece for this, but it wasn't finished in time, though it was later published as No. 3 in his set of organ sonatas, Op. 65.

After returning home, he continued on to Europe, departing from Berlin in May 1831. He went via Dessau to Weimar, where he took leave of Goethe for the last time. After a month in Vienna, he was then absorbed by the art and architecture of the great Italian cities – Venice, Florence, Rome and Naples, returning to Germany in September the following year. This led to his writing the *Italian Symphony*, Op. 90; he directed the premiere at the Philharmonic Society in London, in March 1833. Felix had been quite critical of the music-making in Italy, but nevertheless described this work as 'the jolliest piece I have written so far'.[8] Written for the Royal Philharmonic Society, the symphony was intended to evoke the sights and sounds of Italy, and it uses rhythms of the Neapolitan folk dances, the *saltarello* and the *tarantella*, in the dramatic last movement.

Among the siblings' mutual comments and critiques, Fanny wrote in August 1834: 'Thank you for the symphony movement that just arrived; it gives me great pleasure. I immediately played it through with Beckchen twice . . . But I've digressed from your piece. I don't like the change in the first melody at all: why did you make it? Was it to avoid the many As? But the melody was natural and lovely. I don't agree with the other changes as well; however, I'm still not familiar enough with the rest of the movement to be able to render a reasonable judgement. Overall, I feel you are only too ready to change a successful piece later on merely because one thing pleases you more then. It's always tough, however, for someone to become accustomed to a new version once he knows the old one.'[9]

The *Italian Symphony* is now considered one of Felix's most successful orchestral works, with an exhilarating opening, a delicately scored *Andante*, a picturesque trio in the third movement and a highly original finale, full of vitality. When Fanny included it in one of the Berlin concerts in 1843, she wrote, 'We have had three musical parties at Paul's, and on Wednesday the first subscription concert took place under Felix's direction, with the very beautiful symphony in A major.'[10]

Felix's first public success in Germany was conducting the Lower Rhine Festival at Whitsun in 1833, which his father attended. Abraham wrote to Lea: 'As a music festival comprehends a conductor, I suppose I must say something about the conductor for this year – Mr Felix – he is hardly called anything else here. Dear wife, this young man gives us much joy . . . He has indeed got an immense piece of work to do, but he does it with a spirit, energy, seriousness, and cleverness actually miraculous in its effect . . . By this means he has produced really fine *nuances* both in chorus and orchestra, which all assure me were always wanting before, and which of course gratify the performers and must raise the credit of their execution in their own eyes and ears.'[11] After the Cologne Festival in 1835 the composer and conductor Sir Julius Benedict wrote, 'It would be a matter of difficulty to decide in which quality Mendelssohn excelled the most – whether as composer, pianist, organist, or conductor of an orchestra; nobody certainly ever knew better how to communicate, as if by an electric fluid, his own conception of a work to a large body of performers.'[12]

This achievement at the Lower Rhine Festival resulted in Felix's first paid appointment – from 1 October 1833 as Music Director in Düsseldorf for three years, for 600 thaler[13] a year, which included conducting the choir *Städtischer Musikverein zu Düsseldorf*. Aged twenty-six, from autumn 1835, he became Musical Director in Leipzig; he was the fifth conductor of the Gewandhaus Orchestra. When Robert Schumann discovered the manuscript of Schubert's Ninth Symphony, he sent it to Mendelssohn, who gave the Leipzig premiere on 21 March 1839.

A Chair of Music was founded at Berlin University, with the hope that Felix would fill it, but he was devoted to composing, so declined the offer. He did, however, later spend some time in Berlin, at the request of King Frederick William IV, eventually turning down the invitation to be the Director of Music at the Academy of Arts there. Instead, Felix stayed in Leipzig, returning regularly to Britain.

Queen Victoria wrote in her journal a fine account of their first meeting on 16 June 1842 at Buckingham Palace: 'After dinner came Mendelssohn-Bartholdy, whose acquaintance I was so anxious to make. He is short, dark, and Jewish looking, delicate, with a fine intellectual forehead. I should say he must be about thirty-five or six. He is very pleasing and modest. He played first of all some of his *Lieder ohne Worte*, after which his Serenade and then, he asked us to give him a theme, upon which he could improvise. We gave him two: "Rule Britannia", and the Austrian National Anthem. He began immediately, and really, I have never heard anything so beautiful, the way in which he blended them both together and changed over from one to the other, was quite wonderful as well as the exquisite harmony and feeling he puts into the variations . . . At one moment he played the Austrian National Anthem, with the right hand, he played "Rule Britannia" as the bass, with his left! We were all filled with the greatest admiration. Poor Mendelssohn was quite exhausted, when he had done playing.'[14]

British composer and pianist Charles Salaman described a performance of the Bach Triple Concerto in 1844 with Ignaz Moscheles, Sigismond Thalberg and Felix as 'a trio of giants! And each performer was to play an impromptu cadenza. Moscheles, a famous improvisator, led off with a fine cadence. Thalberg followed with perhaps even more brilliant effect. Then Mendelssohn, who had been leaning listlessly over the back of his chair while the others were playing, quietly began his cadenza, taking up threads from the subject of the concerto; then, suddenly rousing himself, he wound up with a wonderful shower of octaves, indescribable in effect, and never to be forgotten. The audience was so excited that the applause at the end was all for Mendelssohn.'[15]

In 1844 he conducted five of the Philharmonic concerts in London. Writing to Fanny on 13 May 1844 he mentions how, at the Philharmonic, 'my Symphony in A minor was played really splendidly'.[16] In a letter to Rebecka of 22 July that summer he wrote, 'Never before was anything like this season – we never went to bed before half-past one, every hour of every day was filled with engagements three weeks beforehand, and I got through more music in two months than in all the rest of the year.'[17]

Perhaps his greatest musical success in Britain was in 1846, when, on 26 August, he conducted the premiere of his oratorio *Elijah* in Birmingham, to an ecstatic audience of over two thousand. He was quite overwhelmed by the warmth and eagerness of the listeners; writing to his brother, he reported, 'No work of mine ever went so admirably at its first performance, nor was received with such enthusiasm by both the musicians and the audience alike as this Oratorio. No fewer than four choruses and four arias were encored!'[18] Even so, the perfectionist Felix still went on making corrections and alterations.

Felix believed that music was more meaningful than verbal language. While he was also a skilful letter-writer, these two works, the *Overture* and the *Symphony*, tell of his Scottish excursion in a singularly vivid way. The Romantic era made much of programme music; here Felix shows his use of extra-musical ideas as part of his scene painting with musical tones. He once

Sketch of Birmingham by Felix Mendelssohn in a letter from London, 2 October 1840.

stated that 'It is in pictures, ruins and natural surrounds that I find the most music.'[19] Written for the birthday of his friend Heinrich Schleinitz[20] on 1 October 1847, the Eichendorff words of his last song, *Nachtlied*, Op. 71 No. 6, are poignant: 'Gone is the light day / from far comes the bell's tolling / Thus passes the time the whole night / carrying so many along without their knowing.'

Cosmopolitan and acclaimed, even in his maturity, Felix continued to join in with fun and celebration. In Moscheles' diary of 3 February 1847, he reported, 'We and the Schunks[21] had combined to celebrate Mendelssohn's birthday. The proceedings had opened with a capital comic scene between two lady's maids, acted in the Frankfurt dialect by Cécile and her sister. Then came a charade on the word "Gewandhaus". Joachim,[22] adorned in a fantastic wig, played a hare-brained impromptu on the G string . . . She calls her cook – the cook was I myself, and my appearance was the signal for general uproar. Mendelssohn was sitting in a large straw arm-chair . . . and the room echoed with his peals of laughter. The word "Gewandhaus" was illustrated by a full orchestra, Mendelssohn and my children playing on little drums and trumpets; Joachim leading with a toy violin. It was splendid.'[23]

However, friends noticed Felix's decline. In February 1846, Eduard Devrient wrote, 'During these two days that I passed with Felix, I became conscious of the changes that had come over the sources of his inner life. His blooming, youthful joyousness had given place to a fretfulness, a satiety of all earthly things, which reflected everything back differently from the spirit of former days . . . I had remarked lately that he began to repeat himself in his composition; that he began, unconsciously to copy old masters, especially

Mendelssohn on his death
bed, 1847. Sketch by Eduard
Bendemann.

Sebastian Bach, and that his writings exhibited certain mannerisms. I told
him these things, and he received what I said without any irascibility, because
he believed me to be completely in error.'[24]

The entry in the Philharmonic Society records for 1847 reads: 'Dr
Mendelssohn-Bartholdy directed his own compositions, the Scotch
Symphony and the "Midsummer Night's Dream" music. He also played the
Beethoven Concerto for Pianoforte in G, and bade good-bye to the Society,
and to England, alas, as it turned out, for ever. His many friends and admirers
noticed how ill he looked, and learnt with great regret that his lamented
death took place on November 4 of this year.'[25]

Aus frühstem Lebenstraur wie freund linn;
Ruf' Gott Dich ab, bevor Du entunckulen
So geug' Ich hier für mild gemeinem Leben
Und weiter flgendet Dir wie mein

Wilhelm Hensel

6

Fanny

Fanny Hensel had an impressive circle of relatives with artistic connections, and was surrounded by musical, literary and enlightened people, which contributed to the richness of her education, her life and her imagination. She grew to be a highly cultured and discriminating individual, observant of people, art, music and creativity in general. There were notable achievements, but, with hindsight, two frustrations must be articulated – the brevity of her life, and the restrictions on her being published until late in life.

Fanny was the eldest of the four children born to Abraham and Lea Mendelssohn. The day of Napoleon's entry into Vienna was also the day of Fanny's birth in Hamburg, 14 November 1805. Even as a baby she must have had well-matched digits – Lea remarked on her daughter's 'Bach-fugue fingers',[1] which pleased Abraham so much he wrote to his sister in Paris about it. Fanny went on to write over thirty fugues by the time she was nineteen, and, while her compositions were not allowed to be published, those of Felix were, and he became internationally successful.

There is a lot of comparing and contrasting of their music; the connections between their styles are part of their close personal relationship – there was a natural overlap of language and ideas. Felix was the leading German composer of the 1830s and 1840s; his music is often described as technically skilled and including graceful control mixed with romantic fantasy. The fact that Fanny had no public obligation has caused people to consider that she had a more flexible imagination while composing, allowing points of difference between their two styles. A popular misconception was in some people's belief that Fanny wrote much of Felix's music; the only evidence of this is the six songs of hers published in his Opp. 8 and 9 songs. Friends and family knew this, but the public imagined her share of Felix's publications to be much larger.[2] Because of societal limits – gender and class (the Mendelssohns were upper class, principally from maternal wealth) – Fanny did not start to publish under her own name until her last year; and comments on her music are generally about her expressiveness. It all begs the question: what is the 'Mendelssohnian' style?

The Mendelssohn family pursued the goal of assimilation and her parents followed the example of Abraham's younger brother, Jakob, by converting to Protestantism and adopting the name Bartholdy. The children were baptised on 21 March 1816 (possibly not by chance, this was also the birthday of Lea's favourite composer, J. S. Bach).

It is largely thanks to their mother, Lea, that Fanny and Felix were so talented; she was their first teacher. When Lea played, Fanny would come and stand next to the piano. As an advocate for the music of Bach at a time when his compositions were rarely heard, Lea often played the forty-eight preludes and fugues of his *Well-Tempered Clavier*. But Fanny and Felix received a broad education, developing both physical and mental capacities. Their studies embraced foreign languages, ethics and religion, music, drawing, painting and dance. Private tutors were engaged for the boys; the girls' education was a bit less regular, pointing to the attitude that women's position in Prussian society was in the home. Consistent with his times, Abraham would have thought that the only vocation for a young woman was that of a housewife, and the purpose of Fanny's education was to combine knowledge with good manners.[3]

Aged fourteen, Fanny had twenty-four of Bach's '48' by heart, and she played them in honour of her father's forty-second birthday in November 1818. Aunt Henriette (Abraham's sister, known as Jette) wrote to Lea: 'Fanny's wonderful achievement of learning twenty-four Preludes by heart, and your perseverance dearest Leah, in superintending her practising, have made me speechless with astonishment, and I have only recovered the use of my voice to make this greatest success generally known. But with all the intense admiration I feel for both you and Fanny, I must confess that I think the thing decidedly blameable: the exertion is too great and might easily have hurt her. The extraordinary talent of your children wants direction, not forcing. Papa Abraham, however, is insatiable and the best appears to him only just good enough.'[4] Fanny, however, was undeterred.

Journeying to Paris in 1816 with her father, she had some lessons with the pianist Madame Bigot – Marie Bigot de Moroguges had so impressed Beethoven with her sight-reading of the *Appassionata* sonata that he gave her his nearly illegible manuscript, and it is likely that Fanny's great appreciation and playing of Beethoven may have stemmed from Bigot. Later, for about five years, the pianist and composer Ludwig Berger taught her in Berlin. On 1 October 1820 (with Felix), she joined the Berlin Sing-Akademie, led by Carl Zelter. At one point, Zelter favoured Fanny over Felix; he wrote to Goethe in 1816, in a letter introducing Abraham Mendelssohn to the poet, 'He has adorable children and his oldest daughter could give you something of Sebastian Bach. This child is really something special.'[5] Much later, in an 1831 letter to Goethe, Zelter described Fanny's skill as a pianist with the highest praise for a woman at the time: 'She plays like a man.'[6] Starting in 1819 both Fanny and Felix received instruction in composition with Zelter, who laid great importance on understanding counterpoint.

From 1819 the Mendelssohn parents' expectations for Fanny and Felix began to divide; Fanny received a jewel-necklace, where Felix was given writing implements with which he might compose an opera. However, their musical life together as children led to their having common musical projects, naturally sharing their personal musical tastes. Through the events at the Leipziger Strasse house, they promoted works worthy of note, and raised their audiences' expectations.

From March 1820 onwards Fanny started saving her compositions in a music album, which included thirteen French settings of Jean-Pierre Claris de Florian. In 1821, Mozart's youngest son, Franz Xaver Mozart, came through Berlin on a concert tour and privately played duets with Fanny; she won praise from him, even though he was an unusually taciturn person.

On 16 July 1820, Abraham wrote to Fanny a much-cited letter: 'Perhaps for him [Felix] music will become a profession, while for you it will always be an ornament and can and never should become the ground bass of your being and doing.'[7] Despite her choices being constrained by both gender and social class, in the way that devoted musicians have, Fanny fulfilled her public position as wife and mother, while also pursuing her love of music, both as a pianist and a composer, and even as a promoter and conductor.

Italien was one of her *Lieder* of this period (written in the hope of visiting Italy, to a text from about 1825 by the Austrian dramatist Franz Grillparzer). It was later chosen by Queen Victoria to sing with Felix on his 1842 visit to Buckingham Palace – with a little embarrassment, he had to explain that it was written by Fanny, even though published under his name as No. 2 of his Op. 8 in 1826.

Late in 1821, the private concerts in the family residence on the Neue Promenade developed into fortnightly events that Lea called *Sonntags-Übungen* (Sunday practices). These progressed in 1822 to a series of musical matinees; the spacious, central *Gartenhaus* at Leipziger Strasse 3 had space for more people, and the great and the good of Europe came to their house. Thanks to the growing reputation of the concerts, the eminent musicians of the day passing through Berlin requested to be included and came there to participate. Fanny made these salon concerts a forum for her own performing and composing; in time she became a kind of musical director, in managing these events.

Dated 17 March 1825, she wrote a document for promoting instrumental music in Berlin;[8] she included remarks on the only other classical music institution in Berlin, run by the violinist and composer Karl Möser, who presented a Berlin concert series between 1813 and 1843 (they included the Beethoven String Quartet Op. 132, in 1828). Fanny thought that the series did little to captivate audiences with new and unusual features. She demonstrated her independent mind in comments on programming (setting her sights on symphonic music), publicity and remarks about women not appearing before

Opposite. Wilhelm Hensel,
self-portrait, 1829.

an audience. In this practical essay, there was a brief account of costs, plans for membership fees, a lending library and a public series of twelve subscription concerts. Meanwhile, the Sunday matinees grew in importance and extent over the years; along with the salons and the opera, they made an important contribution to Berlin's cultural life.

In 1821, Fanny met the artist Wilhelm Hensel (1794–1861) at festivities honouring the visit of the Grand Duke Nicholas Pavlovich; these included Hensel's representations of Thomas Moore's poem of Eastern romance *Lalla Rookh*, which were designed as *tableaux vivants*.

Hensel left for Italy in 1825, commissioned by the King of Prussia, Frederick William III, to make copies of Raphael's *The Transfiguration*, and to make his own original painting to serve as an altarpiece.[9] While he was away, Lea forbade letter-writing; she didn't want Fanny longing for him in his absence. Nonetheless, slightly ironically, it was Lea who replied to Wilhelm when he attempted to correspond with her daughter. Instead, Fanny wrote songs about loss, distance, absence – her *Sehnsucht* ('Yearning', H-U 340) song of 1826 is beautifully sad. From Rome, Hensel sent drawings of the Mendelssohn family, before returning to Berlin in 1828. His paintings, shown at the September annual exhibition at the Royal Academy of Art in Berlin, resulted in Frederick William III appointing him as the Prussian court painter.

Fanny's feelings for Hensel survived the separation. He made his way back into the Mendelssohn family circle, and the couple were engaged in January 1829. They married on 3 October at the Parochialkirche Berlin, which was filled with relatives and friends. Felix had planned to write music for the nuptials, but was delayed in London by an accident, so Fanny wrote her own wedding music; they processed and recessed to her Prelude in F, and Postlude in G; regardless of any chauvinistic attitudes, her music was at last heard in a semi-public place. In a letter to Felix she wrote: 'Father had suggested the *Pastorelle* for the recessional, but I couldn't find it . . . Then, around 9 o'clock, Hensel suggested that I compose a piece, and I had the audacity to start to compose in the presence of all the guests. I finished at 12.30 and don't think it's bad . . . It's in G major; I already knew the [key] because I had earlier devised one before you promised to send me one. But the style is conservative.'[10]

Aware of society's narrow view of female creativity, Fanny wrote to Wilhelm shortly before their marriage: 'I am composing no more songs, at least not by modern poets I know personally . . . I now comprehend what I've always heard and what the truth-speaking Jean Paul has also said:[11] Art is not for women, only for girls; on the threshold of my new life I take leave of this plaything.'[12] Fortunately, Wilhelm rejected this bleak plan, and insisted that she continue with her art.

Notwithstanding his own limited musical ability, Wilhelm was supportive of her composing and her works continued to be performed at the Sunday

Wilhelm Hensel
und
Fanny Hensel,
geb. Mendelssohn-Bartholdy.

musicales. Apparently he said he wouldn't marry Fanny unless she carried on writing music, and every morning of their marriage, before he went off to paint, he would put a piece of blank manuscript paper on her music stand and tell her he wanted to see it filled when he returned.[13] Towards the end of her life Fanny received an enquiry as to whether she was the author of *Auf Flügeln des Gesanges*[14] ('On Wings of Song'); she wrote to Felix, 'In general, I'd like to send a list of my pieces that are floating around the world concealed. It seems they're not even clever enough to separate the wheat from the chaff.'[15]

In 1825, Karl Klingemann was working as a clerk in the Hanoverian legation, on the second floor of the Leipziger Strasse house, and gave Fanny the recently published *Hammerklavier* sonata, Op. 106, by Beethoven. He even wrote an imaginary letter from Beethoven to Fanny, dated 8 November 1825: 'My most worthy *Fräulein*! Reports of your efforts on my behalf have reached as far as Vienna . . .'[16] From this letter we know that Fanny had Beethoven's 4th and 5th piano concertos and the *Archduke* trio in her repertoire.

Abraham's birthday greetings to Fanny in November 1828 included a letter with his usual encouragement to prepare for her 'real calling, as a housewife'.[17] Wilhelm celebrated the event with a different offering: a pair of ornamental shears and this poem:

According to the sage
a shear cuts off life's threads.
So you grasp the special question,
Why I gave you the shear.
More than a crown or sceptre
it should speak of the sacred power
that often assigns to you
the threads of my life for all eternity.
To remain, wander, live, or die
in exile or the fatherland,
to lose hope and regain it –
all rest henceforth in your hand![18]

To create an outlet for her musical self, which would not conflict with her role as wife and mother, Fanny reinstated the (somewhat diminished) Sunday musicales around the beginning of 1831. She arranged the programmes, composed much of the repertoire, played the piano and organised a small choir which she rehearsed on Friday afternoons. Her 1825 proposal had mapped out her idea 'to establish an instrumental music lovers' association . . . [as] this declining art needs a strong hand to raise it, otherwise it will disappear in the bad taste of the time, the egotism of the organiser, and the

pandering of the public.'[19] Some of her most ambitious works were composed
for these occasions.

At Christmas 1828, Wilhelm gave Fanny a miniature Florentine album
in the shape of a heart, inscribed 'This little book is very like the heart, / You
write in it joy or sorrow'.[20] This romantically shaped diary includes a couple
of touching entries by Wilhelm about her pregnancy; the sketches depict a
child with an attendant angel-like fairy, the protecting spirit fending off a
sinister bat, while the infant lies awake in a flower. Their son Sebastian was
born two weeks prematurely, on 16 June 1830; he not only survived, but later
wrote about the legacy of this extraordinary family in his book *Die Familie
Mendelssohn*. In the diary, Fanny also recorded musical sketches, while
Wilhelm added poems and drawings of important events in their lives.

During the winter of 1838 there was regular music at Leipziger Strasse 3,
which brought an opportunity for Fanny to perform Felix's Piano Concerto
in G minor (Op. 25). Her pianistic public debut was as his deputy on 19 February 1838 at a concert at the Berlin *Schauspielhaus*.[21] The press lauded her
performance; without identifying her by name, they made comments such
as – 'excellent dilettante, intellectually and naturally related to the
composer'.[22]

Animated by the success of her Sunday musicales, she wrote to Klingemann, 'Last week the fashionable world was in great excitement about a
charity concert – one of those amateur affairs where the tickets are twice the
usual price, and the chorus is composed of countesses, ambassadresses, and
officers. A woman of my rank was of course pressed to play, so I performed
in public for the first time in my life . . . I was not the least nervous, my friends
being kind enough to undertake that part of the business for me, and the
concert, wretched as the programme was, realised 2,500 thalers.'[23]

She also wrote to Klingemann about the difficulties she encountered:
'Once a year, perhaps, someone will copy a piece of mine, or ask me to play
something special, certainly no oftener; and now that Rebecka has left off
singing, my songs lie unheeded and unknown. If nobody ever offers an
opinion, or takes the slightest interest in one's productions, one loses in time
not only all pleasure in them, but all power of judging their value. Felix, who
is alone sufficient public for me, is so seldom here that he cannot help me
much, and thus I am thrown back entirely on myself. But my own delight in
music and Hensel's sympathy keep me awake still, and I cannot help considering it a sign of talent that I do not give it up, though I can get nobody to
take an interest in my efforts.'[24] Possibly Felix was so absorbed in his successful
life that he didn't really consider how Fanny felt. Wilhelm's solution to
Fanny's sense of isolation was to encourage her to publish.

Of course, the publishing matter was not simple. Abraham and Felix both
thought it was wrong for her to issue her music in public. With hindsight,
we can observe the gender conventions of those days with concern regarding

the restrictions and what good music has been lost. Writing to Felix, Fanny expressed her thoughts: 'With regard to my publishing I stand like a donkey between two bales of hay. I have to admit honestly that I'm rather neutral about it, and Hensel, on the one hand is for it, and you, on the other, are against it.'[25] Reminiscent of the fable *Buridan's Ass*, unable to decide which way to go, the ass ends up starving.

Instead, she once again made the Sunday musicales in the *Gartenhaus* at Leipziger Strasse 3 her chief focus of attention and, with some pauses, continued to hold these until her death. The concerts, which had begun a few years earlier as musical entertainments for gatherings of friends and relatives, changed impressively over this time. According to Sebastian Hensel, they assumed larger and larger proportions as regards the performers, the audience and the character of the music. Many of the visitors were total strangers brought by persons themselves only recently introduced; the rooms became so overcrowded that the musicians could scarcely find standing room, to say nothing of sitting. They became very prestigious events, with royalty or visiting musical celebrities as part of the audience.[26]

Early in 1837, Fanny sent a song to the music publisher Schlesinger, who issued it. Felix wrote from Leipzig, 'Do you know, Fance, your song in A major in Schlesinger's Album is a grand success here? The new *Musical Gazette* (I mean the Editor, who dines at the same hotel with me) is quite enthusiastic about you. They all say it is the best thing in the album – a bad compliment, for nothing else is good. But they really appreciate it. So now you are a real author, and I hope you feel pleased.'[27]

Opposite. Sebastian Hensel. Pencil drawing by Wilhelm Hensel, 1860.

7

The Italian Journey

After the Napoleonic wars, there was a new wave of travel to the south. Not only was Goethe a family friend, but they all knew well his *Italienische Reise* (*Italian Journey*, 1817).[1] Fanny was also familiar with Heinrich Heine's philosophical and political essay series *Reisebilder*, and the poet Wilhelm Müller had published a summary of Italian travelogues in 1821.

In Goethe's art-loving Weimar, Italy was considered the New Jerusalem.[2] Near the end of his Italian journey, and about to leave Rome, he wrote, 'the sun is shining and I can see a paradise . . . One is made aware of the multiplicity and diversity of human forms and brought back to man at his most authentic, so that the beholder himself is more human and authentic'.[3] In 1817 Abraham had planned a family trip to Italy, but it didn't come about; instead the household went to Switzerland for four months in 1822. Felix visited Italy in 1830; one of his sketches, *Die Spanische Treppe* (*The Spanish Steps*), came from that expedition. The Prussian Consul in Rome, their uncle Jakob Bartholdy, lived in Casa Bartholdy near the Steps, and it was partly through Fanny's correspondence with him that Italy remained in her thoughts. In the end, Wilhelm's love of Italy and Fanny's desire to go meant that her wish was finally realised in 1839; the Hensels set off on 27 August for their year's journey southward, with their nine-year-old son Sebastian and Jette the cook.

Prior to leaving Berlin, Fanny wrote in her diary: 'Let God grant us a good journey without mishaps and always good news from home, and He should let us find everything unchanged, then shall we experience a wonderful time. I am looking forward to this big event with quiet joy; let it be a good omen. Amen!'[4] In good German Romantic tradition, all the Mendelssohn family were accomplished letter-writers, and Fanny's travel reports include rich descriptions of their Italian experiences, alongside the family chatter. Throughout her year away Fanny also kept a travel diary, so, along with the correspondence to the family, there are accounts of what they did and the people they met, as well as discussions on buildings, artworks and the landscapes they saw.

The journey began (and ended) with a visit to Felix and family in Leipzig, following which they left the city on 4 September 1839 by horse-drawn coach,

Opposite. The Campo Vaccino, Rome, by J. M. W. Turner. In a letter to Felix, Fanny wrote that 'Nature and time have converted the imposing buildings of the Romans into a heap of ruins, the charm of which, however, is unparalleled'.

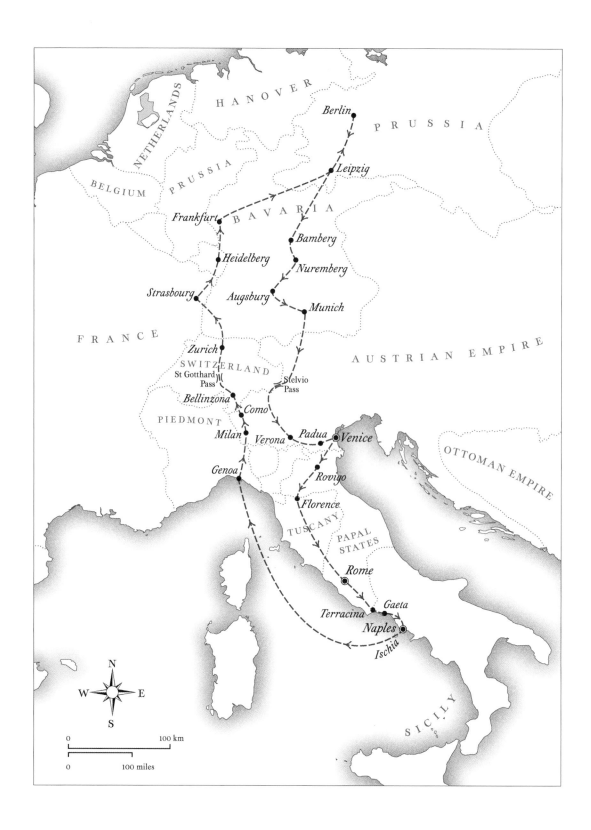

HANOVER

PRUSSIA

Berlin

NETHERLANDS

BELGIUM

PRUSSIA

Leipzig

Frankfurt

BAVARIA

Bamberg

Heidelberg

Nuremberg

Strasbourg

Augsburg

Munich

FRANCE

Zurich

SWITZERLAND

AUSTRIAN EMPIRE

St Gotthard
Pass

Stelvio
Pass

Bellinzona

Como

PIEDMONT

Milan

Verona

Padua

Venice

OTTOMAN
EMPIRE

Genoa

Rovigo

Florence

TUSCANY

PAPAL
STATES

Rome

Gaeta

Terracina

Naples

Ischia

SICILY

N
W E
S

0   100 km

0   100 miles

travelling through Bamberg, Nuremberg and Augsburg to Munich. On 24 September they crossed the Alps via the Stelvio Pass and, having arrived on the Italian side, Fanny wrote to her mother: 'I have never seen anything so wild and deserted-looking as this summit . . . splendid road, bordered by rocks, in a steep ascent . . . real alpine scenery . . . surrounded on all sides by glaciers.'[5] It was spectacular, beautiful and cold. With the undeveloped modes of transport of the early nineteenth century, the whole excursion was a major undertaking, as well as wish-fulfilment.

The great Classical history of Italy had drawn visitors to see its art and architecture for centuries. As the source of civilisation, Fanny already knew much about Italy, its literature and paintings, as well as details from Felix's earlier journey. A letter of his from Rome in December 1830 reported that the orchestras were worse than anyone could believe and that no improvement could be hoped for. 'Why should Italy still insist on being the land of art, while in reality it is the land of nature, thus delighting every heart!'[6]

After crossing the Alps, Fanny was thrilled by the southern scenery and subtropical vegetation – citrus fruits, roses and fig trees; they went via Verona

Opposite. Map of the Hensels' Italian journey, September 1839–September 1840.

Above. Sketch by Felix Mendelssohn of the Spanish Steps in Rome, 1830–31.

Venice, by J. M. W. Turner. Fanny wrote that 'one scarcely knows which to admire most, its grandeur or its fairy-like beauty'. The Hensels spent three weeks there.

and Padua (which 'left a disagreeable impression of decay')[7] to Venice, which she loved. On 12 October 1839, they boarded the postal ship at Mestre for the six miles to Venice, soon enjoying the Byzantine marvels of St Mark's Basilica. After approaching Venice by water she wrote, 'one scarcely knows which to admire most, its grandeur or its fairy-like beauty . . . I do not remember in my whole life to have felt so much astonishment, admiration, emotion and joy in any twenty-four hours as I have in this wonderful city.'[8] The Hensels spent three weeks in Venice, often referring to Goethe's 1786 *Reise*; despite Fanny wanting to find her own way around, Felix's advice was given anyway. While there, she composed the Venetian *Serenata* in G minor; later renamed *Gondelfahrt*, it was like a Venetian barcarolle.

The Hensels left Venice on 4 November in foul weather. After Rovigo they found the River Po overflowing, thanks to continuing rain, and were delayed by the flood; the following day they moved on (paying twenty-six *paoli* instead of the regular charge of three to cross the river), and arrived in Florence on the 7th.[9] They visited churches and admired the paintings of Tintoretto and Veronese, and were full of the joys of Titian, most notably the painting of *Flora* – 'as much like a goddess as a scamp'.[10] Fanny then described the onward carriage journey: 'During the whole way from Florence to Rome I said each day at nine o'clock, what a monotonous and wearisome road this is! At ten o'clock, how charming! By eleven it was again dull; at twelve once more beautiful, and so on for the whole six days. That is the peculiarity of this country: you are in a constant state of either delight or of disgust.'[11]

The Hensel family reached their goal – the Eternal City – at night on 26 November 1839. As Wilhelm planned to spend the winter there, they rented an apartment on Via del Tritone for six months. They soon joined the German community and Fanny was made much of by the circle of German artists and the French Fellows of the Académie gathered at the Villa Medici, which at that time housed the winners of the Prix de Rome, France's most prestigious musical prize.

The Prix de Rome was initially created for painters and sculptors in 1663 in France, during the reign of Louis XIV. It was an annual bursary for promising artists who proved their talents by competing in a very difficult elimination contest. The first musical prize was established in 1803, in which year Napoleon Bonaparte moved the *Académie* to the Villa Medici, with the intention of preserving an institution once threatened by the French Revolution. The Villa was a splendid, late sixteenth-century palace, but not in good order; it had to be renovated to house the winners. In this way, Napoleon hoped to give the young French artists the opportunity to see and copy the masterpieces of antiquity and the Renaissance. Among the Prix de Rome scholars that Fanny met were the painter Charles Dugasseau and the composer Georges Bousquet, whom, in 1840, Wilhelm sketched along with Charles Gounod.

Charles Gounod, who won the Prix de Rome in 1839 with the composition of his cantata *Fernand*, became a great admirer of Fanny both as a pianist and as a composer, and encouraged her to publish. Remembering the music at the Villa Medici, he wrote later in his memoirs: 'Mrs Hensel was an extremely learned musician and played the piano very well. Despite her small, slight figure she was a woman of excellent intellect and full of energy that could be read in her deep, fiery eyes. Along with all this she was an extremely talented pianist. She had rare powers of composition, and many of the *Songs without Words* published among the works and under the name of her brother were hers.'[12] The warm reception and Gounod's admiration awakened new creative powers in Fanny: 'Now I am writing a lot; nothing spurs me on like praise, whilst censure discourages and depresses me.'[13]

Meeting the prize winners (*pensionnaires*) in Rome, Fanny was struck by the different ways of the French people – their lightness and ability to respond

Tante Grazie
per il ritratto
D il N° 2.

Charles Gounod

Il ne manque à mon portrait que
la parole, pour pouvoir dire à cet illustre
artiste qui en est l'auteur combien je suis
heureux de l'avoir connu. — Ne m'en veuillez
pas, M. Hensel, si j'ai mal posé c'est
Mad.e Hensel et le N° 1 qui en sont en
grande partie la cause.

A. G. Bousquet

Roma. Villa Medicis 31 mai 1840.

Merci à M.r Hensel pour mon
beau portrait, à M.me pour les délicieux
moments que j'ai passés chez eux tout
à moi n°3 qui a été la cause
première de ces deux plaisirs.

Dupré Lévêque

Rome 31 Mai 1840

to new circumstances contrasted with the rather staid ways of the German colony there. The relaxed spontaneity of the French affected her, and her normally serious side began to be complemented by more outgoing tendencies; she learned that taking it easy did no harm to her creative side.

Wilhelm renewed contact with old acquaintances in Rome, who eased their access to the galleries, and they met some of Felix's friends from his earlier visit. They watched Pope Gregory XVI process with the cardinals into the Sistine Chapel. The Holy Father was suspicious of reforms, and banned railways, using a French pun to dismiss them as *chemins d'enfer* (infernal roads), not *chemins de fer* (iron roads).[14]

The Hensel couple soon connected with the music-making in the city, but Fanny wrote about the performances in St Peter's Basilica as being 'far from perfect'[15] and further commented that the music in Rome was not up to the standard of the *Sonntagsmusiken* that she had organised at home in Berlin. The French painter Jean-Auguste-Dominique Ingres (from whom we get the phrase *le violon d'Ingres* owing to his passion for playing the violin) was the director of the Académie Française at the Villa Medici from 1835 to 1841 and, on 7 December 1839, he invited Fanny and Wilhelm to dinner, after which they moved to the music room and played trios. Following this, they spent many Sunday evenings making music in this congenial environment.

At these Sunday concerts, Fanny introduced the French visitors to her German repertoire: Bach, Mozart, Hummel, Beethoven, and works by her brother and herself – all new to them, and the audience became her fervent admirers. Her diary recounts a May evening when she played Beethoven's *Les Adieux* sonata and parts of *Fidelio*, followed by a walk to the Colosseum and the Trevi Fountain in glorious moonlight.

Gounod was particularly full of praise for Fanny: 'Thanks to her great gifts and wonderful memory, I made the acquaintance of various masterpieces of German music which I had never heard before, among them any number of works of Sebastian Bach and many of Mendelssohn's compositions, which were like a glimpse of a new world to me.'[16] He later came to Berlin near the end of April 1843, staying nearly a month with the Hensels and, demanding that Fanny play for him, he hardly left the house, even though she wanted to show him the city.

In Rome, during February 1840, Wilhelm was ill with a stomach ailment for several weeks and unable to work, but reported that Fanny was an excellent nurse. However, by the time of the effervescent Carnival near the end of that month he had recovered, and everyone lost themselves in the exuberant merrymaking. The Hensels loved the festive event; it took place in the bustling streets, in the narrow thoroughfare that ran from the foot of the Capitoline Hill to the Piazza del Populo, the ceremonial entryway to Rome. Fanny knew about the Carnival from Goethe's description: 'at a given signal,

Opposite. The three Prix de Rome scholars, Gounod, Dugasseau and Bousquet, whom the Hensels met in November 1840. Sketch by Wilhelm Hensel, 1840.

Bartolomeo Pinelli's painting of a Roman carnival, 1834. Fanny described the carnival at length in her letters.

everyone has leave to be as mad and foolish as he likes, and almost everything, except fisticuffs and stabbing, is permissible'.[17]

He chronicled the events in the *Corse* (horse races, carriages, promenaders), the *Commedia dell'Arte* costumes (many Pulcinelle), the laughing at lawyers and Quakers, the masks and fancy dress, men dressed in women's clothes.[18] Candles were important: '*Sia ammazzato chi non porta moccolo*' ('Death to anyone who is not carrying a candle') was said to others, while trying to blow out their candle. Goethe had also commented that 'life, taken as a whole, is like the Roman Carnival, unpredictable, unsatisfactory and problematic.'[19] Fanny might also have known Bartolomeo Pinelli's 1834 etching *Carnival Costumes*, or his son Achille Pinelli's (1835) *Scene of Rome's Carnival*.

The week of events included races, games, dances and general merriment; the revellers hurled hard confetti at each other (sugar-coated almonds used as petty warfare), and it all culminated in a special evening of candles: the *moccoletti*. 'I am far more amused with it all than I expected . . . Goethe

described it fifty years ago . . . The missiles, *confetti* (made of plaster of Paris) are returned in kind, and Sebastian was quite indignant with me for sending a bouquet in reply to a volley of *confetti*, because I had nothing else to hand.'[20] Fanny's writings illustrate how much she enjoyed the colourful events and the exuberant, southern energy; she wrote to her mother: 'Do you recognise your daughter, frolicking away for hours in the midst of this turmoil, and in a noise which can be compared neither to the roaring of the sea nor to the howling of wild beasts, being like nothing but itself?'[21] Alongside her serious, cultured persona, Fanny clearly liked being playful and joining in the fun. To everybody's astonishment, snow fell in Rome on 25 March,[22] and, because of Wilhelm's illness in February, they delayed their departure until 2 June.

Fanny returned to composing early in 1840, producing an a cappella trio for Lea's birthday (on verses from Goethe's *West-östlicher Divan*), plus three piano pieces and a cavatina for voice and piano, H-U 348, on a text from Ariosto's *Orlando furioso* (1516). The admiration she received from the Sunday concerts gave her a new confidence, as expressed on 26 April 1840:

'It will cost us both a hard struggle to leave Rome; I could not have believed that it would have made such a deep impression on me. I must not conceal from myself that the atmosphere of admiration and homage in which I have lived may have had something to do with it, for even when quite young I never was made so much of as I have been here, and nobody can deny that this is very pleasant.'[23]

Fanny visited St Peter's and had a poor opinion of the music there, but much enjoyed the spectacle of the variety of costumes in the crowded church. On the morning of Good Friday she sat for three hours in the Sistine Chapel, listening to unpolished and mediocre singing, including the singers losing pitch (she herself had perfect pitch). Her short-sightedness may have restricted her visual appreciation, but the pomp of the papal ceremonies impressed her: 'Of course there is no expression at all . . . These obsolete forms of singing remind me of ancient mosaic, but they strike me as even more stiff and death-like . . . in the Sistine, where art has been carried to the culminating point of perfection, and where, in consequence, the utter poverty of the music is felt to be the more incongruous.'[24]

Near the end of their time in Rome, on 20 May 1840 at the Villa Wolkon- sky,[25] the Hensel couple organised a party worthy of Boccaccio's *Decameron*, with painting and drawing, singing of part-songs in the open air and playing games. Fanny wrote a song, *La Tristesse*, on some verses by Alphonse de Lamartine, for soprano and tenor. In the piano piece *Ponte Molle* (the Milvian Bridge, composed in May 1840) she expressed her heartache over leaving Rome; it was the last station travellers met when entering or leaving the city.

Their stay in Rome had been a great success, both for Wilhelm and his art, and for Fanny and her music-making. They supported each other's creative efforts and he often painted vignettes on her manuscripts. They were sad to leave; her diary of Saturday, 30 May mentions that after packing 'I was very tired and low, so to prevent myself beginning to cry again I went to the piano and played the two Allegros from Beethoven's Sonata in F minor.'[26] In her diary she reports that she played several Beethoven sonatas and concertos.

Overall, their six months in Rome were some of the happiest times of Fanny's life. On 17 May 1840 she wrote in her diary: 'All these experiences have made me younger instead of older. Such a tour as this is a treasure for life.'[27] Her last diary entry in Rome concluded: 'And a wonderful, lovely, rich time has passed! How can one thank God for two months of uninterrupted bliss! The purest enjoyments of which a human being's heart is capable of have followed each other, almost no disturbing quarter-of-an-hour the whole time, no pain except that time has expired. The final farewell from St Pietro in Montorio was not easy for us. But I have an eternal, imperishable picture in my soul, which will never fade. I thank you, oh God!'[28]

Leaving Rome, they moved southwards; after Terracina[29] the vegetation grew more luxuriant and southern, including cypresses and palm trees. The Hensels arrived in Naples on 1 June, and although the summer heat restricted them a little, their time became more holiday-like after the busy social round in Rome. Their apartment had a magnificent view of the Bay from the balcony, and Fanny spent many happy hours on it, possibly remembering the famous saying 'See Naples and die',[30] quoted by Goethe.

They took the steamer to the volcanic island of Ischia, covered in profuse, wild greenery, and drove by carriage to the foot of the volcanic Mount Vesuvius on 16 June (Sebastian's birthday), then made the almost perpendicular ascent by horseback and sedan chairs. Vesuvius was described by Goethe as 'the hellish cauldron',[31] and they gazed in astonishment and horror at the crater, with its sulphurous smells, before stumbling back in darkness, and finding their horses to carry them to their accommodation at the Hermitage. Following the experience of the Caldera, Fanny's visit to the remains at Pompeii was also filled with wonder. Another excursion on donkeys and boats took them to Capri.

In a July diary entry, she wrote, 'Oh, you beautiful Italy! How much have you enriched me! What an incomparable treasure do I carry home in my heart!'[32] They had made several excursions from Naples; but with the heat, she decided that Wilhelm should go off alone to Sicily, on the steamer. Notable among her compositions from this journey was her *Schwanenlied*, a fine union of great poetry and expressive music; she chose this as the first song of her Op. 1, the collection she published in 1846.

After nearly three months in Naples, on 11 August 1840, they set off on the four-day boat journey to Genoa, then travelled homeward by coach via Milan, Zurich and Lucerne, back to Felix in Leipzig, and arrived home in Berlin on 11 September. The concluding entry of her travel diary states, 'Of the impression made upon me by our return home I will write at some future period, when the present has become the past, and the storm has either passed over our heads or expended its force upon us. I have learnt from experience that there are subjects which it is best not to deal with at the time.'[33]

According to Seneca, 'Travel and change of place impart new vigour to the mind.' After the provincial limits of Berlin society, the Italian journey changed Fanny's life through its considerable and different collection of experiences; she was growing into a new maturity and self-assurance, which she used to enliven further composing. This was a year of fresh incidents and adventures, of art, of people, of discovering southern landscapes and of unusual appreciation, which refreshed her substantially. Before the Italian journey, she'd been writing less music, not least because of the time and energy required to organise the *Sonntagsmusiken*. But while abroad she composed *Lieder* and piano works, and then, after a year of absorbing the experience, she wrote *Das Jahr: 12 Charakterstücke für das Forte-Piano*.

8

Das Jahr

People often choose music as the medium for celebrating special times and events, such as Christmas and Easter, and the seventeenth-century composer Christopher Simpson wrote a set of twelve pieces, one for each month of the year, entitled *Months and Seasons*. Haydn named three of his early symphonies after different times of the day: *Le Matin*, *Le Midi*, *Le Soir*. Later, Franz Liszt composed his *Années de pèlerinage* as representations of his travels; and Tchaikovsky's *The Seasons* were published in 1886. Fanny Hensel composed her *Das Jahr: 12 Charakterstücke für das Forte-Piano* (*The Year: 12 Character Pieces for the Piano*) during the last four months of 1841, from 28 August to 23 December. Although her journey had begun in September, she kept to traditional chronology and began her cycle with January, naming each piece after a month of the year, with an added postlude.

In a genuinely Romantic musical cycle, the whole became a vivid synthesis, a triple-counterpoint of musical, literary and visual imagery. Hensel contributed vignettes to the top-left corner of each new piece; interleaved between each month, they also included epigrams by Uhland, Goethe, Schiller, Eichendorff and Tieck. Thus, the total expression of the work was deepened. Altogether, they evoke the passage of time and the seasons of human life, a narrative of change, some tinged with a wistful sense of loss. This ambitious series places short piano works in a new sphere, through the elaborate web of ideas, of musical depiction and musical connections.

The painstaking care that Fanny and Wilhelm lavished on *Das Jahr* underscores its central significance in her *oeuvre*; arguably, it is her most impressive achievement. Aged thirty-six, she had produced a major piano composition that dramatically expanded the scope of the short piano pieces she had hitherto composed. The twelve *Charakterstücke* were no longer separate, but a sequence of movements meshed together by related musical (such as an overarching key plan) and extra-musical elements (poetry and art). It is clear that Fanny crafted the individual movements with large-scale effects in mind.

People sometimes set the music of Fanny beside that of Felix; considering that the siblings were nurtured in the same music environment, family similarities would be expected. Occasionally the comment that her language was like his makes it sound as though she copied him – an attitude that has reduced appreciation of her individuality; she was more than three years older, and naturally the musical style of the time was used by both composers. The grace and clarity of Felix's music makes a distinctive contrast with her more fervent emotional expression, and while the siblings had a rare mutual understanding, they each had their own distinctive approach and manner; his music featured polish and beauty, whereas her communication had more intensity. *Das Jahr* reveals the strength of her musical language and style.

The twelve pieces feature a coordinated sequence of keys: sharp keys are favoured in the first half, progressing more and more to flat keys, arriving at C major for December, with A minor for the coda-like *Nachspiel*, and ending with a *tierce de Picardie* (major chord). Fanny strengthened the links between adjacent pieces through harmonic means: January begins in B major and ends in C sharp minor; these keys act as subdominant and dominant to the key of February, F sharp major. That key is where March begins, and then concludes in C sharp major. June's D minor links to its relative major, F, for July. January and February, and April and May, are bound together by the instruction *attacca*; by continuing without a pause, the listener perceives them as related parts of the annual cycle. The scope of the whole is impressive, as well as the range of emotion and idea in the music (from the thoughtful chorales to the brilliant, agile music of, for example, January).

Das Jahr is significant as an autobiographical document; Fanny described her piano pieces as 'a kind of second diary',[1] and it has a wider expression in being about time as it continues. As well as the spiritual rituals of the year, there are changes of the seasons, evoked by weather; other natural imagery is found in the poetic texts that accompany particular movements. Bells also mark the passing of time, such as in the repeated quavers of the prelude to March. The original manuscript added another dimension: colour – each month was written on paper of different hues, from cream to dark brown. The tones of the paper for the individual movements seem to have been chosen for their expressive qualities. Pastel shades were preferred for spring; June's blue might evoke an evening serenade; yellow-to-brown indicated the hotter months; and November, the onset of winter, is on a darker brown.

Wilhelm's vignettes and the epigrams link closely; indeed, the relationship between music, epigram and drawing are sometimes quite complicated, with the textual and visual elements helping to clarify the meaning of the music. Illuminating all of this (and contributing substantially to this commentary), Marian Wilson Kimber drew up an extensive description of the relations between the words, drawings and the music in *Fanny Hensel's Seasons of Life: Poetic Epigrams, Vignettes, and Meaning in 'Das Jahr'*.[2]

The vignette for January includes three winged cherubs holding bells flying overhead; the bells are symbolic of marking the passing of time, and the *putti* (cherubs) take after those in Raphael's *The Marriage of Cupid and*

Fanny Hensel's manuscript of *Das Jahr*, January, with vignette by Wilhelm Hensel, 1840. The bells held by the cherubs are symbolic of the passing of time.

Psyche, where the figures are *Horae* (the *Hours*). Many of Wilhelm's drawings suggest that the story is generally being told from a woman's point of view, such as the woman in July, who resembles a tired pilgrim. Almost half the drawings focus on a single woman, and others have larger groups. Several of the epigrams include imagery depicting nature's yearly changes, and it feels as though Fanny and Wilhelm viewed *Das Jahr* as a joint effort. This is all in keeping with the Mendelssohn family beliefs about the relationship of music and text, as well as the evocation of extra-musical associations known in Hensel's circle.

There are two other possible influences on the general form. Firstly, Austrian dramatist Ignaz Franz Castelli's texts *Die zwölf Monate, An die Frauen* ('*The Twelve Months, To the Women*') set to music by German composer

Johann Heinrich Karl Bornhardt, and published about 1828–9. Its depiction of the seasons often had similarities with the epigrams and Hensel's approach in *Das Jahr*, mostly obviously with September as a hunting scene and November with harsh winds. Secondly, Johann Christian Friedrich Schneider's *Die Jahreszeiten* ('The Seasons', written in the early 1820s), based on poems focusing on nature by T. L. A. Heinroth, set for between one and four voices and piano. Although these pieces both come from composers of an earlier generation, there are few stylistic resemblances with Fanny's music.

Haydn's *Die Jahreszeiten* ('The Seasons') is a more noteworthy influence. Fanny's father, Abraham, was fond of Haydn's oratorios, from their combination of religious impulses with nature. Furthermore, Felix owned some of the original sketches for the *Seasons* oratorio.[3] In 1804, Zelter wrote an extensive review for the *Allgemeine musikalische Zeitung* (the foremost German-language music periodical of its time) and the Sing-Akademie performed it in 1830. Moreover, Fanny's letters (27 December 1835 and 14 December 1838)[4] relate that she had heard performances of the oratorio. Just as Haydn's overture dissolves into the next season, so the introductory octaves of Fanny's January recall the opening descending minor tetrachord of *Die Jahreszeiten*. October and Haydn's *Landvolk und Jäger* chorus (No. 26) share material, such as four rising semi-quavers leading to a horn-call figure. November's middle section characterises winter weather in a similar way to Haydn's recitative and Aria No. 38.[5] In both, winter is a metaphor for death; libretto and vignette are connected through the grave. The oratorio's final chorus calls on God to provide strength and courage, with similar sentiments being invoked in the *Nachspiel*'s chorale tune ('The old year has passed'); Fanny's design points to her thinking beyond nature, to life itself.

Both Fanny and Felix regularly composed works as gifts for family members, and *Das Jahr* was written as a birthday present for Wilhelm; the musical remembrance made a very special offering. Dedicated to him, she wrote:

> To the man who, for many a year,
> As long as I have been with him
> Shortened them for me to perpetual holiday
> Gave zest for life with poetry,
> To him, the serious, able one is presented
> The glittering picture of the fleeting year.[6]

The epigrams included in *Das Jahr* came from several different poets; most were from Goethe (five), with three coming from his *Faust*. As well as knowing him personally, the Mendelssohns were of course familiar with his writings. Goethe not only mentored Felix, but also gave him a bifolio from *Faust*, Part Two, in 1830. Fanny had already set his *Erster Verlust* in 1821, and then met him in 1822, sometimes quoting him in her letters. More than for their authorship, the epigrams were chosen for their content.

Fanny's letter to the painter Friedrich August Elsasser (11 November 1841) said, 'Now I am making another small work, with which I'm having much fun, namely a series of twelve piano pieces meant to represent the months, I'm already more than half done, when I'm finished I'll make clean copies of the pieces, and they'll be provided with vignettes.'[7] It is not clear exactly when the epigrams came into the overall plan, and it is not possible to know if they were an inspiration or an afterthought; looking for autobiographical references yields little of a specifically personal nature. Yet correspondence between text and music can be found in the poetry from which the epigrams come. In MS 47 in the Mendelssohn Archive, January is marked *Ein Traum* ('A Dream'), which suggests that Fanny may have been influenced by the poet Ludwig Uhland's *Im Herbste* ('In Autumn'), the source of that epigram; the lines just before are 'Even from Yonder garden halls / I hear joyful chords resound'. Garden halls may refer to Fanny's joyful chords in her *Sonntagsmusiken* in the *Gartenhaus* at home, or her *Das Jahr*.

Wilhelm's accompanying vignette for January portrays a woman with a psaltery, apparently depicting Fanny with the musical instrument symbolic of her creative talents.[8] This first piece mixes adagio and presto in a clearly improvisatory manner suggestive of setting out on a journey, and thoughtful searching develops into joyful excitement. The very opening, descending octaves have been linked by Christopher Alan Reynolds[9] to *Es ist Vollbracht*[10] from Bach's *St John Passion*, representing the expression of grief.

The music carries on *attacca* into February – this scherzo seems to evoke the exuberance and celebration of the Roman Carnival (thus, the nearest to the biographical interpretation). Chromatic scales in octaves punctuated by chords could represent the pelting of plaster confetti; however, the epigram suggests a larger literary carnival – in *Faust* Part Two (1831), lines 5065–8, the Herald's speech features a parade of allegorical figures, which in turn suggests the carnival of life. In *Italian Journey* Goethe wrote that the Carnival reminds us of 'the most important scenes of life'.

Further in the letter to Elsasser, Fanny seems to reconcile losing the past with living in the present and not knowing what the future will bring. This coming to terms with life and the changes time brought can be related to creating a piece like *Das Jahr*; perhaps it is even a musical expression of life's transience, its joys and sorrows. The letter to Elsasser continues, 'Thus we seek to decorate and beautify our lives, that is the preference of artists, that they strew such embellishments round about themselves, and can let all who stand at all near them take an interest in it.' Fanny and Wilhelm shared life, art and time; they were intertwined, and the passing years were expressed through art.

A bigger picture comes from looking at the full poems from which the

Das Jahr, February. Hensel's vignette depicts the Roman carnival.

epigrams were taken. For example, the two sections of fast semiquavers in April can be seen to represent the snow in Goethe's poem *März* (from four lines earlier than the section from which the epigram is taken); Wilhelm's vignette shows a woman protecting a baby from some undesirable weather. The full source of the May epigram gives more of an idea of Fanny's design: while the lyrical, pastoral music fits the epigram about the blossoming of spring, the refrain at the end of the two stanzas urges the poor heart not to be afraid, and to forget the torment, as all must change.[11] This movement connects with themes in later movements (June and August), foretelling what is to come, reinforcing the cyclical nature of the year. The *dream* of the spring to come is also the composer's dream of the whole piece.

March's epigram is taken from Faust's speech in Part One (lines 744–5), when he hears the muffled bells announcing the first ceremony of Easter. The music is written on purple paper, and contrasts a well-voiced prelude with a chorale of grandiose splendour, which gradually gets 'filled-in', and

Das Jahr, March, with its vignette of Easter.

more integrated with the prelude's music. Fanny quoted the Lutheran chorale *Christ ist erstanden* ('Christ has risen') – a four-part chorale by Bach (BWV 276) concerning the resurrection; this hymn is possibly the oldest Christian liturgical German song. Semiquavers lead to a great climax, with the chorale tune in the left hand, which refer both back to the bells of the previous movement and forward to the arrival of Easter. The epigram further amplifies the unsung resurrection text 'Christ is risen', and the section of *Faust* preceding the epigram has a chorus singing *Christ ist erstanden*.

April is capricious, contrasting graceful and spirited ideas, and leads straight into May, an optimistic, 9/8 spring song. June appears in two versions, sharing key, meter and general character, but there are differences. The first version (MA MS 47) is nocturne-like, with a Chopinesque introduction, gradually leading to a climax featuring three-hand texture, with the melody played between the two thumbs. The second version has no suggestion of virtuosity and is formally straightforward. In MA MS 155, Wilhelm's vignette of a man serenading with a lute suggests love fulfilled more than Faust dancing with witches (less in common with the epigram then in this month). Possibly Fanny thought the first version too evocative of Faust's ascent of the Brocken mountain – too literal a depiction would undermine the more universal programme she desired. The second version's general consistency and regular cadences downplay Faust's climb to the vulgar celebration among the supernatural. The texts that surround the epigram express that time has passed, the love song is merely memory; the nocturnal blue music-paper suggests what has been.

Fanny's use of *Faust* epigrams did not follow their order in the original Goethe. The February epigram comes from the second part of *Faust*, while March and June's are from the first. Other epigrams resonate with the emotional turmoil of Faust, such as that for July which includes *der Mensch verschmachtet* ('People languish') from a Friedrich Schiller poem, and September's *Nimmer wird ich froh* ('Never will I be happy') from Goethe. Fanny's year, therefore, is not simply an account of developing joy and fulfilment: April features capricious snow, June has lost love songs and September senses continuing unhappiness. These are understandable if Fanny's music depicts more than the mere chronology of months; it is nearer to wishing. If the epigrams are Faustian, then it is about striving towards fulfilment.

July suggests the languor of heat, and includes the rumbling of a thunderstorm, possibly followed by raindrops. The epigram for August refers to the harvest and is taken from Schiller's poem *Das Lied von der Glocke* ('The Song of the Bell'), in which descriptions of the casting of the bell alternate with the story of a lifetime; the bell's role is to teach that all earthly things fade away. This literary context suggests not just the harvest as the culmination of the growing season, but the larger cycles of life. The music is joyous and exuberant; it starts with a fanfare wake-up call, followed by a pastoral march – again being on the move. The next epigram, two lines from Goethe, elucidates Hensel's vignette (a barefooted woman by a stream): 'By the river, flow, flow, / Never will I be happy.'[12] On deep turquoise paper, September ripples on the river (*am Fluss*), with a wash of brooding semiquavers, which have a slightly autumnal feel. This lays the ground for the flourishes and horn calls of October, a hunting scene.

Ludwig Tieck's poem *Trauer* provided the epigram for the dark, dramatic November; however, Fanny changed his original wording *Liebe* to *Leben*, from 'the dreams of *love*' to 'the dreams of *life*'. About more than the coming of winter, and on dark brown paper, the vignette shows a priest holding a shovel next to a tombstone, an image recalling the liturgical place of All Saints' Day at the beginning of the month. The dismal opening could be thought to be a funeral march; if it's a metaphor for death, then it's the death

Das Jahr, September, with its
semiquavers suggesting
ripples on water.

of life's dreams. The *mesto* tempo heading for November might mean sad
or heavy, or both, but Fanny's *agitato* energy will out once more.

The epigram for December is *Vom Himmel hoch, da komm ich her* ('From
heaven above, I come to earth'), a hymn text relating the nativity of Jesus,
written by Martin Luther in 1534. Bach had set the first stanza in his 1723
Magnificat and used the melody three times in his 1734 *Christmas Oratorio*.
Fanny's piece starts with a *leggiero* shimmer, expectant excitement leads in
time to the hymn tune, framed by magnificently contrapuntal music.

This all prepares the chorale of the *Nachspiel* – a simple thanksgiving,
full of chromatic nuances; *Das alte Jahr vergangen ist* is a reflection on the
'year' that has just passed, as well as alluding to Bach's *St Matthew Passion*,
BWV 244.[13] The text of the chorale is fitting – thanking God for his care and
praising Him. December and the *Nachspiel* have the same-coloured paper,

Das Jahr, December, a celebration of the Nativity.

and there is no epigram for the *Nachspiel*, which suggests that Fanny thought of the two sections as linked. The *Nachspiel* reference to the opening procession music of the *Passion* evokes the procession of years, as one year turns into the next. The whole set combines to suggest the passage of time, the seasons of human life.

Das Jahr can be set beside Robert Schumann's *Carnaval*,[14] from four years earlier, in which members of that composer's circle (Clara Wieck, her father, Chopin and others) make memorable appearances, all in the context of carnival time; in contrast, Fanny compresses her carnival into the one month of February, but manages to represent herself, Wilhelm and Felix. Her use of three chorales can be connected to Felix's cultural project of the Bach revival, as well as her own religious convictions. However, there are a variety of other overall interpretations. *Das Jahr* has been read as related in detail to her

Italian sojourn, as well as given elaborate structural analysis,[15] and even considered as absolute music with no autobiographical expression, despite the clearly descriptive titles.

Her three chorales (March for Easter, December for Christmas and *Nachspiel* to mark the passing of the year) link the series to Protestant Berlin, and most notably show her connection with Felix. The cycle is told from Fanny's perspective: in the January vignette, she reclines with her left hand resting on a cithara (a symbol of musical inspiration). The four lines from Ludwig Uhland's *Im Herbste* confirm her dream:

Ahnest du, o Seele, wieder	O soul, do you discern again
Sanfte, süsse Frühlinglieder?	Soft, sweet songs of spring?
Sieh umher die falben Bäume,	Look about you at the dun-coloured trees
Ach! es waren holde Träume	Ah, it was a lovely dream

This is not the hopeful renewal of spring; Fanny initiated a fantasy-like dream sequence, with hints of material from February, April, June and August, validating the dream/reverie as an overall topic for the cycle. Frequent tempo shifts suggest the idea that the whole is about the perception of time – real time, spiritual Christian time and free-associative, subconscious time. February's epigram quotes Hector in the second part of Goethe's *Faust*:

Denkt nicht, ihr seyd in deutschen Gräntzen,
                       Do not think you are in German lands
Von Teuffels- Narren- und Totendtänzen
                       with the dances of devils, fools and death
Ein heitres Fest erwartet euch
                       a merry feast awaits you

February could be related to such dancing; this is the month of Rome's carnival, and is a joyful, exuberant scherzo, hinted at by Goethe's epigram quoted above. In the vignette, Wilhelm serenades Fanny, who is listening to him from a balcony. She wrote two versions, the second featuring the rhythmic ambiguities of hemiolas, barcarolle lilting and a three-hand effect. It concludes with the chimes of the great clock tower announcing morning.

Although it's less clear that other family members play a role in the cycle, Felix features through unmistakable references to his music. February recalls material from his *Rondo capriccioso*, Op. 14 (June 1830), March quotes from the *Serenade und Allegro giojoso*, Op. 43 (1838), April is a reworking of his *Capriccio brilliant*, Op. 22 (1832) and June adapted his first *Gondellied* (1830).

Finally completed in December 1841, the cycle was given as Wilhelm's Christmas present. Below are details and composition dates of each of the movements:

Detail of the vignette for
February, which features
Fanny on the balcony (left),
being serenaded by Wilhelm.

January: A Dream. Adagio quasi una fantasia – Presto. 11 December 1841
February: Scherzo – Presto. 28 August 1841
March: Agitato. 17 November 1841
April: Capriccioso – Allegretto. 7 October 1841
May: Spring Song – Allegro e giocoso. 16 October 1841
June: Serenade – Largo. 29 October 1841
July: Larghetto. 9 November 1841
August: Allegro. 15 November 1841
September: At the River – Andante con moto. 15 November 1841
October: Allegro con spirito. 1 December 1841
November: Mesto. 4 December 1841
December: Allegro molto. 16 December 1841
Postlude: Chorale. 15 December 1841

• • •

On 21 February 1842, the English composer William Sterndale Bennett wrote to a friend: 'I went to a small music-party at Mendelssohn's, where I met all his family and some other people. He played three pieces and then insisted on my playing. I never was so alarmed before; not at him, for we have played too often together, but at his sister, Mrs Hensel . . . I never was frightened to play to anyone before, and to think that this terrible person should be a lady. However, she would frighten many people with her cleverness.'[16]

In a letter to her sister, Rebecka, of 18 March 1844, Fanny wrote about a particularly showy *Sonntagsmusik*: 'We had twenty-two carriages in the court, and Liszt and eight princesses in the room . . . [However, I will] dispense with my describing the splendours . . . but I will give you my programme: quintet by Hummel, duet from *Fidelio*, variations by [Ferdinand] David, played by that capital little [Joseph] Joachim, who is no infant prodigy, but a most praiseworthy child, and Sebastian's great friend to boot . . .'[17] Otherwise, Felix was arranging a performance of Handel's oratorio *Israel in Egypt* with 450 performers, while preparing his orchestra for Beethoven's Ninth Symphony. At about this time, Fanny tells Rebecka: 'Now that I am getting so near forty, I think how young and lively I mean to be when I am fifty.'[18]

In 1846, Fanny met diplomat and pianist Robert von Keudell. Her diary of 17 May noted, 'Another agreeable acquaintance is Herr v. Keudell, who has such an ear for music as I have not met since Gounod and Dugasseau, plays extremely well, and is altogether a very lively and charming man.'[19] He visited daily and grew intimate with Fanny's music; his support played an important role in convincing her to begin publishing under her own name and he provided the same encouragement she had received in her earlier relationship with Gounod. Of von Keudell, she wrote: '[He] keeps my music alive and in constant activity, as Gounod once did. He takes an intense interest in everything that I write, and calls my attention to any shortcomings; being generally in the right too.'[20]

Both Abraham and Felix had discouraged Fanny from making music in full view of all. For an upper-class German woman of that period to enter the domain of public music in that way would have lowered her social standing. She had mixed feelings about publishing, but it would appear that she saw presenting her compositions more openly as an important step in artistic fulfilment. Possibly Felix's lack of enthusiasm for Fanny to publish came from thinking that publishing required a string of new compositions. However, on 9 July 1846 she wrote to Felix to report that she had decided to publish, moving independently, in order to spare him any unpleasantness.[21]

Songs had been central in her creations, so she started by presenting several *Lieder*, and by the end of the month she had competing offers from two well-established Berlin firms, Bote & Bock, and Schlesinger. She recorded in her diary, 'Bote & Bock have made offers to me the likes of which have perhaps never before been given to a dilettante composer of my sex, whereupon Schlesinger even outdid them. I do not in the least imagine that this will continue, but am pleased at the moment, having decided to embark on this course, to see my best works appear in print.'[22] Lea urged Felix to approve and, despite his earlier coolness, he finally gave his blessing in a letter of 12 August 1846: 'I send you my professional blessing on becoming a member of the craft . . . may you have much happiness in giving pleasure to others; may you taste only the sweets and none of the bitterness of authorship.'[23]

The title page of Fanny's fair copy of *Das Jahr* suggests her aspiration to produce it publicly, since it proudly states: *Das Jahr: Zwölf Charakterstücke für das Fortepiano von Fanny Hensel*. Furthermore, engraver's markings are notated on the first autograph, which imply that there was a plan to publish. However, it was never published in her lifetime; instead, somehow the manuscript came into the possession of a representative of the Lord Mayor of Baden-Baden. Pianist Ayako Suga-Maack gave the first performance of the complete cycle in November 1997 (the 150th anniversary of Fanny's death), the same year that the National Library in Berlin purchased the manuscript for its Mendelssohn Archive, and Furore Verlag published a facsimile edition of the fair copy in 2000.[24] At least three movements exist in different versions (June), or with significantly revised passages (August and December). September was published by Fanny in her Op. 2, but without the title 'September'.

Fanny was encouraged by the success of her publishing venture. Her diary entry of February 1847 reads: 'It is enticing to have this manner of success at an age when such pleasures, for women who experience them at all, are usually at an end.'[25] Inspired by this fulfilment, she began to compose a larger-scale piece – the Piano Trio in D minor, intended as a birthday present for Rebecka. It premiered on 11 April 1847 at a Sunday musicale, with von Keudell playing the violin and her brother Paul the cello, where it 'was received with universal applause'.[26] In 1847, an anonymous critic for the *Neue Berliner Musikzeitung* wrote, 'We find in this Trio, broad, sweeping foundations that build themselves up through stormy waves into a marvellous edifice. In this respect the first movement is a masterpiece, and the Trio most highly original.'[27] The music is passionate, and the piano part illustrates that she must have been a very agile and expressive pianist. It is an enthralling work, with torrents of notes pouring from the piano complemented with sonorous string lines. Both the middle movements are poetic and beautiful, while the finale, starting with a piano cadenza, takes ideas from Bach and gypsy music. Breitkopf & Härtel published it in 1850 as her Op. 11, and today it is probably her most played work.

✝ 14. Mai 1877.

9
Legacies

On 11 December 1842, Abraham's birthday, Lea suffered a stroke and died. Fanny wrote, 'it was as she would have wished – to depart suddenly from the middle of the life she loved, in full possession of the intellectual brilliance always her lot in life'.[1] Fanny prayed that God would grant her such a death; in the end, there were similarities – she also died of a stroke (aged forty-one), as did Felix (aged thirty-eight). Apoplexy occurred in the Mendelssohn family with some regularity, and there seems to have been a genetic component; grandfather Moses, the parents and the two sisters died from similar attacks. The type of stroke suffered by the Mendelssohn family is thought to be a subarachnoidal haemorrhage.[2]

Fanny's last song, *Bergeslust* ('Mountain Passion'), was finished on 13 May 1847; on a text by Joseph von Eichendorff, the final line is: 'Thoughts and songs are borne heavenward.' The next day she was rehearsing Felix's *Die erste Walpurgisnacht* when she lost sensation in her hands, retired to bed and died that evening. When given the news, Felix fell on the floor in a faint. He was devastated, and wrote to Wilhelm: 'If the sight of my handwriting checks your tears, put the letter away, for we have nothing left now but to weep from our inmost hearts, we have been so happy together, but a saddened life is beginning now. You made my sister very happy, dear Hensel, through her whole life, as she deserved to be. I thank you for it today, and shall do as long as I live, and longer too I hope, not only in words, but with bitter pangs of regret, that I did not do more myself for her happiness, did not see her oftener, was not with her oftener. That would indeed have been for my own pleasure, but it pleased her too. I am still too much stunned by the blow to be able to write as I would: still I dare not leave my wife and children and come to you, knowing as I do that I can bring neither help nor comfort. Help and comfort – how different these words sound from all I have been thinking and feeling since yesterday morning. This will be a changed world for us all now, but we must try and get accustomed to the change, though by the time we have got accustomed to it our lives may be ended.'[3]

The Sing-Akademie held a memorial celebration for her on 18 May; also on that day, the *Vossische Zeitung* published an obituary by the poet Ludwig Rellstab. Clara Schumann remembered her fondly, and the English music

Opposite. Fanny Hensel on her deathbed, 1847.

83

critic Henry Chorley wrote in *The Athenaeum*: 'Had Madame Hensel been a poor man's daughter, she must have become known to the world by the side of Madame Schumann and Madame Pleyel, as a female pianist of the very highest class. Like her brother, she had in her composition a touch of that southern vivacity which is so rare among the Germans. More feminine than his, her playing bore a strong family resemblance to her brother's in its fire, neatness and solidity. Like himself too, she was as generally accomplished as she was specially gifted.'[4] It's striking that her reputation was known in London at that time. For Wilhelm, her death represented 'the loss of everything, for the whole family life was destroyed',[5] and, according to Sebastian, he never painted anything worthwhile in the fifteen years that he survived her.[6]

Felix was shattered after Fanny's death, and, in a kind of atonement for withholding support previously, he took some of her manuscripts to his publisher, Breitkopf & Härtel, pursuing publication with more energy. Devrient described Felix as living his final months under the 'impending sword of the angel of death',[7] and in this mood he wrote the intense F minor String Quartet, Op. 80, in her memory. The East German scholar Georg Knepler later called it the '*Requiem* of an era'.[8] Felix was so upset by the loss of his favourite sister that he couldn't survive long without her, and he died on 4 November 1847, aged just thirty-eight. The public were allowed to see Felix's body on the 5 and 6 November in Leipzig. The pallbearers included Moscheles, Robert Schumann and Niels Gade, and his funeral was held at the Paulinerkirche, Leipzig, attended by the great and the good of the musical world. The coffin was transported by rail to Berlin and he was buried in the Trinity Church Cemetery No. 1 in Berlin-Kreuzberg.

On 11 November 1847 the Gewandhaus concert was made up entirely of compositions by Felix. The Sacred Harmonic Society in London performed his *Elijah* on 17 November, and commemoration concerts were given in Berlin, Frankfurt, Vienna, Hamburg and other cities. Letters of condolence came from numerous people, including the Queen of England, the King of Prussia and the King of Saxony.

The Swedish soprano Jenny Lind had become a great friend, after they met in London in 1844, and Felix had started writing the opera *Die Lorelei* for her in the last months of his life (three numbers were completed and published posthumously in 1852 as his Op. 98). Lind gathered singers familiar with his *Elijah* for a performance at Exeter Hall on the anniversary of his death, at which *The Times* noted her approach was 'rendering art subservient to a higher purpose than display . . . a rare gift . . . But Madame Jenny Lind possesses it in a remarkable degree'.[9] The concert raised the remarkable sum of a thousand pounds for a Mendelssohn Foundation.

Upon Felix's death, Lind wrote: '[He was] the only person who brought fulfilment to my spirit, and almost as soon as I found him, I lost him again.'[10]

In 1849, she established the Mendelssohn Scholarship Foundation, which makes an award to a young resident British composer every two years in Mendelssohn's memory. In 1869, Lind erected a plaque as a Mendelssohn commemoration at his birthplace in Hamburg.

The funeral of Felix Mendelssohn, Leipzig 1847, from the *Illustrated London News*.

Clara Schumann said, 'My recollections of Mendelssohn's playing are among the most delightful things in my artistic life. It was to me a shining ideal, full of genius and life, united with technical perfection. He would sometimes take the *tempi* very quick, but never to the prejudice of the music. It never occurred to me to compare him with virtuosi. Of mere effects of performance, he knew nothing – he was always the great musician, and in hearing him one forgot the player, and only revelled in the full enjoyment of the music. He could carry one with him in the most incredible manner, and his playing was always stamped with beauty and nobility. In his early days he had acquired perfection of technique; but latterly, as he often told me, he hardly ever practised, and yet he surpassed everyone. I have heard him in Bach, and Beethoven, and in his own compositions, and shall never forget the impression he made upon me.'[11]

One of his obituaries noted, 'First and foremost we esteem his pianoforte-playing, with its amazing elasticity of touch, rapidity, and power; next his scientific and vigorous organ playing [...] his triumphs on these instruments are fresh in public recollection.' Mendelssohn once described death as a place 'where it is to be hoped there is still music, but no more sorrow or partings'.[12]

•   •   •

Comparing CDs and books about them, today Felix has roughly four times as many as Fanny. While there is a growing interest in women composers, even now they do not have the same exposure as their male counterparts.

Thanks to his many opportunities, Felix composed a much wider range of works than Fanny achieved. His life included the stimulation of being a professional musician, hearing his compositions played by others, having them published and the invigorating experiences of travelling abroad. In his short life he wrote a broad range of works, including symphonies, concertos, chamber music, piano pieces, choral works, church music and songs.

While fulfilling her home-based duties, Fanny composed a substantial number of pieces, particularly music suitable for her Sunday musicales. Felix ranked Fanny's songs as among the very best German examples of the time, and the *Allgemeine musikalische Zeitung* wrote in 1847 that she allowed her fantasy 'a freer rein' and applied form 'with broader brush strokes'. Her songs are now her most appreciated works, but she also wrote cantatas, a fine string quartet and the above-mentioned *Piano Trio*.

People sometimes link her music to that of Felix, but I think they are very different. As the cellist Pablo Casals said, Felix was 'a romantic who felt at ease within the mould of classicism'; Fanny's compositions by contrast are awash with emotion. Primarily in memory of Felix, the Mendelssohn Foundation honours his memory and gives prizes for remembering his creativity.

Some two centuries later, we can look at the siblings' lives and achievements with the benefit of changed social views. Fanny's recently rediscovered *Easter Sonata* was broadcast by BBC Radio 3 on International Women's Day 2018, and there are over forty CDs which include her music. While people know her name, few are actually familiar with her compositions, but she is now receiving more of the recognition she deserves.

In May 2009, BBC Radio 3 chose to devote their programme *Composer of the Week* to Felix and Fanny together, suggesting that while he was long appreciated, she was also now coming into the limelight.

Felix's extraordinary precocity (described as exceeding that of Mozart) could be said to have worked against him later in life, and some people believe that he had peaked by his later teenage years. Robert R. Reilly, in 'Mendelssohn – Great or Also-Ran?', mentioned that Brahms noticed the condescension toward Mendelssohn that became typical during the latter half of the nineteenth century when he would simply respond, 'Yes, yes, Mendelssohn, he was the last of the great masters.'[13] In terms of public knowledge and appreciation, Felix had a huge advantage over Fanny through having so much of his music published. His Wedding March is played very frequently, possibly without people knowing the composer's name, and his oratorios continue to be popular with choral societies. The elegance and charm of his music account for much; he fitted the Romantic artist cliché of dying young; he had a warm relationship with the Philharmonia and an impressive connection with Queen Victoria; and is now considered as one of the first significant Romantic composers.

Felix's performance of Bach's *St Matthew Passion* is today thought of as the primary impetus for the modern Bach revival; Felix played organ pieces by Bach in St Paul's Cathedral in 1829 and 1832; and later in his life he prepared an edition of Bach's organ works, published in London by Coventry and Hollier, 1845–6. In making Bach's music available to a wider public, he has undoubtedly contributed to the widespread recognition and appreciation that Bach has today.

Referring properly to both Fanny and Felix, the adjective 'Mendelssohn-ian' has been used to describe the music of composers Felix influenced, such as William Sterndale Bennett, Robert Schumann, Neils Gade and Johannes Brahms. The *Leipziger Ausgabe der Werke von Felix Mendelssohn-Bartholdy* is published by Breitkopf; and Bärenreiter issued the twelve volumes of *Briefe*[14] in 2008. At the end of the nineteenth century, the city of Leipzig erected a monument to Felix, near the St Thomas Kirche, and although Wagner made some antisemitic attacks on him, his music in now being better researched and played. American Mendelssohn scholar R. Larry Todd credits his subtle influences on other composers and genres, from Schoenberg, to Ives, to Irving Berlin and even Heavy Metal.[15]

His historical reception has included being lionised, attacked, neglected and rehabilitated. In the twentieth century the Nazi regime and its *Reichsmusikkammer* cited Felix's Jewish origins when banning performance and publication of his works, even asking Nazi-approved composers to rewrite incidental music for *A Midsummer Night's Dream* (Carl Orff obliged). After the Third Reich's efforts at effacing him from the German musical canon, his music has been universally enjoyed again.

Around 750 of Felix's works still remained unpublished in the 1960s, but most have now been made available. A complete scholarly edition of his works and correspondence has taken many years to complete, and is in excess of 150 volumes. All of Mendelssohn's *oeuvre* – including the most popular works, such as the E minor Violin Concerto and the *Italian Symphony* – has been explored more deeply, and prior concepts about the Victorian conventionality of the oratorio *Elijah* have been shed. The frequently intense and dramatic world of Felix's chamber works has been more fully recognised, and virtually all of his published works are now available on CD, and frequently heard in the concert hall and on broadcasts. As the critic H. L.

Fanny Hensel's music room,
by Julius Helfft, 1849.

Mencken concluded, if Felix indeed missed true greatness, he missed it 'by a hair'.[16]

The position of women in the nineteenth century however, and Fanny's fewer publications, meant she was less in the public eye. There was some unease in evaluating the work of a woman composer who was the sister of an international celebrity, and her early death and the revolution of 1848 led to neglect of her compositions until towards the end of the twentieth century, when she was recognised as a great *Lieder*-writer. In 1850, the distinguished Leipzig firm had, though, published her last works: *Vier Lieder für das Pianoforte* (Op. 8), *Sechs Lieder* (Op. 9), *Fünf Lieder* (Op. 10) and the Piano Trio (Op. 11); the latter work now being among the most popular piano trios by women, and quoted as one of her major achievements. In the twenty-first century her songs feature in *Lieder* recitals and there are some thirty CD recordings of her music, including songs, piano pieces and cantatas. Her compositions have been catalogued by Renate Hellwig-Unruh[17] – they number up to H-U 466 – and the German publisher Furore Verlag has now issued many of them.

Although the press generally made little comment on Fanny's living activities, on the occasion of her death, the poet and music critic Ludwig Rellstab described her as an extraordinary musician who had played a vital role in the musical life of Berlin, and her home as 'the sacrificial altar for worshipping the best in music. That is a service for the artistic standard of our city for which we are deeply obliged.'[18] In June 1847, the *Allgemeine musikalische Zeitung* reviewed her published piano music and, while commenting on

Felix's precise manner, they said, 'Frau Hensel's *Lieder* are more complicated; here fantasy is permitted freer rein, the form is applied in broader strokes, and not infrequently a greater variety is achieved by means of a contrasting middle section.'[19]

In 2007, Sony Music released a CD of *Das Jahr*, played by Lauma Skride, which was reviewed by *The Gramophone* as a 'valuable and rewarding addition to this genre of the literature'; and by *BBC Music Magazine* who said, 'a seam of dignified melancholy runs through it; we find a raw emotional intensity that is uncommon in Felix's music. The work is an excellent example of Fanny Hensel's unsurpassed lyricism, delicate humour and splendid virtuosity.'

Throughout the years, it has been difficult for Fanny Hensel to escape from her brother's penumbra – the principal biography (by R. Larry Todd) has the subtitle 'The Other Mendelssohn'. A Duke University Symposium in 1989 included a paper by Paula Higgins entitled 'In Her Brother's Shadow – The Musical Legacy of Fanny Mendelssohn Hensel'. The *Kapralova Society Journal* has a substantial article by Eugene Gates entitled 'Fanny Mendelssohn Hensel: A Life of Music within Domestic Limits'. Some writings about her add the words '*geboren* [born] Mendelssohn' and since in the nineteenth century it was customary to take the married name, 'Mendelssohn' therefore mostly belongs to Felix.

Wilhelm offered a brief eulogy: 'Her life was truth; her end blessed'.[20] In this commentary about travel, it is notable that her final work told of leaving home. She was buried in the cemetery of Trinity Church, Berlin, near her parents, and where Felix joined her some months later. In 1861, Wilhelm was interred there too, bringing together in death the people who sustained Fanny in life. Her tombstone was later inscribed with a quotation from her final song, *Bergeslust*:[21]

> Oh joy, to look around from the hilltop
> Far across woods and stream,
> under the deep blue vault
> rising crystal-clear above us.
>
> Down from the hill-tops birds
> and clouds are flying so swiftly,
> our fantasies easily taking over
> the birds as well as the wind.
>
> The clouds are sinking down,
> The bird glides down alike, [but]
> Our fantasies as well as our songs
> Rise up until they reach heaven.

THE LETTERS

The Falls of Braan, near Dunkeld. Sketch
by Felix Mendelssohn, 2 August 1829.

The Letters

In August 1829, following his success in London, Felix travelled north, for the three-week visit to Scotland; resulting in two of his best-loved pieces, the *Hebrides Overture* and the *Scottish Symphony*. Life was very different in Scotland's mountainous world and wild weather; at a latitude some 4 degrees north of Berlin, it was also a good deal colder. Blair Atholl, where the first letter was written, was a small village in the Cairngorms and Felix's description of the storm suggests he is both fascinated and horrified, though he is also taken with the country people. Inventive as ever, he comes up with a new way of drawing. This is his first big journey and the final paragraph shows he thinks of home.

Opposite. Birnam Wood, near Dunkeld. Sketch by Felix Mendelssohn, 4 August 1829.

From Felix to Abraham Mendelssohn: Blair Atholl, Evening, 3 August 1829. Highland inn at the bridge of Tummel

A wild affair. The storm is howling, blustering, and whistling around outside, causing the doors to slam shut down below and blowing the shutters open, but one can't tell whether the sounds of water are from the rain or from the blowing spray, since both are raging. We're sitting here calmly around the burning hearth, which I poke a bit from time to time, making it flare up. Otherwise, the room is large and empty, water is dripping down along one of the walls; the floor is thin, and the conversation in the servants' quarters can be heard echoing up from below; they're singing drunken songs and laughing – dogs are barking as well. Two beds with purple curtains, on our feet Scottish wooden shoes instead of English slippers, tea with honey and potato cakes, a narrow winding staircase, which the maid made use of to bring us whiskey, a dismal procession of clouds in the sky, and in spite of all the wind and water noises, in spite of the servants' conversation and the banging doors it seems quiet! Quiet and very lonely. I should like to say that the quiet resounds even through the noise. Just now the door opened by itself. It's a Highlands ale house. The little boys with their plaids and bare knees and colourful caps, the waiter in his tartan, old people with their periwigs, all speaking a jumble of incomprehensible Gaelic.

The countryside is broad and wide, covered with dense vegetation, from all sides cascades of water are rushing under the bridges, there is little corn but much heather with brown and red flowers, ravines, passes, crossroads, everywhere beautiful green, deep blue water – but everything is stern, dark and very lonely. How could I describe it? Ask Droysen,[1] who knows it well and can paint a better picture than I, we are always quoting lines from his *Hochlands* to each other. Now I am addressing him: Dear Droysen, did you come to know Scotland? It is just as you said it would be.

The weather is discouraging. I have invented my own method of drawing it and today rubbed in some clouds and drew grey mountains in pencil; Klingemann is rhyming cheerfully and I carry out more of the details when it rains. Today is almost an autumn day. I think of how this piece of paper will be carried out to the *Gartenhaus*,[2] and how yesterday at the waterfall the beginning of the letter blew out of my sketchbook and went fluttering down onto the gravel (we scrambled after it and retrieved it though), and how just now the innkeeper's wife is singing her child to sleep with a sweet melody in a minor key, and how all of this is on its way to you.

When the autumn weather sets in, I'll put on my coat for the last day of the journey home and walk in one evening. It will be merry. But now I am still in Scotland and the winds are blustering wildly. Good night, I'm going to my bed inside the red curtains. Sleep well. Felix MB

Felix and Fanny always showed each other their music, thus, the manuscript included in Felix's letter of 7 August 1829 was his way of sharing his thoughts with her; it was normal that he should send her the opening bars of his new *Overture*. Only four days later he describes both his being seasick and many activities. Despite illness, he has sketched a lot of drawings.

On one of the Hebrides, 7 August 1829

In order to make clear what a strange mood has come over me in the Hebrides, the following occurred to me:

[*Some twenty bars of manuscript of the opening of the* Hebrides Overture, see pp. 30–31]

Glasgow, 11 August

How much has passed in the meantime. The most horrible seasickness, Staffa, scenery, travels, people; Klingemann can describe them, for in the first place he didn't have to make the London mail, as I did today, for which I had to write several letters, and second he hasn't been plagued as I have been by severe headaches all evening, which make it hard for me to think, let alone write. Then take into account that it's already midnight, and we've already filled a whole day of our Highland journey with boat travel, galleries, churches, steam, people, and smokestack funnels, and you will excuse me for being so brief. I can't go on today.

Also, the best thing I have to report can be found in the above lines of music, and I'll gladly spare you the description of my illness, the thoroughly unaccommodating damp weather, and so on. So please forgive me this time. I am drawing assiduously, and Klingemann's poems are coming along splendidly, and I also think that several of my pictures were more successful than usual. And expenditures have been more moderate than I thought. We've only spent twenty-four pounds so far. Tomorrow we're going to Loch Lomond and Ben Lomond, to Loch Katrine, the Trossachs, Aberfoyle, Stirling and Lanark. Send some good letters. Pardon this poor, hasty letter and farewell. F

In 1835 Felix became Director of the Leipzig Gewandhaus Orchestra and he worked to develop the town's musical life. Abraham died in November that year, while Lea lived on for another seven years. In March 1837 Felix married Cécile Jeanrenaud and they went on to have five children.

The siblings had had a highly cultured education together. Fanny was fascinated by Felix's travels and longed to explore as well. The opportunity to do a Grand Tour with her husband finally came in the autumn of 1839. Hearing of Fanny's plans to visit Italy, Felix was keen to tell her all about his previous journey round Italy. Leaving in May 1830, he had travelled via Venice and Florence to Rome; in his letter to Fanny he shows impressive artistic understanding and memory. What might seem, to modern ears, slightly bossy instructions could also convey that he didn't want Fanny to miss any of the pleasures he had enjoyed; this is the closely connected conversation that the siblings valued so highly. They were both familiar, of course, with Goethe's *Italian Journey*. Having visited Felix in Leipzig, the Hensels left on 4 September and arrived in Munich on the 10th.

From Felix: Leipzig, 15 September 1839

Dear Fanny,
Wishing to note down a great many things for your benefit, I examined my diaries, but found very little in them, and say to myself, 'Hensel will show her and tell all this a hundred times better than I can.'

So only with a view to perform my promise:
Isola Bella[3] – Place yourself on the very highest point, and look right and left, before and behind you, the whole of the island and the whole of the lake are at your feet.

Venice – Do not forget the Casa Pisani,[4] with its Paul Veronese, and the

Manfrini Gallery, with its marvellous 'Cithern Player'[5] by Giorgione, and a ditto 'Entombment'[6] by Titian (Hensel laughs at me). Compose something in honour of the 'Cithern Player'; I did so. When you see the 'Assumption of the Virgin',[7] think of me. Observe how dark the head of Mary – and indeed her whole figure stands out against the bright sky; the head looks quite brown, and there is an ineffable expression of enthusiasm and overflowing felicity, that no one could believe without having actually seen it. If you don't think of me, too, at sight of the golden glory of the sky behind Mary, then there is an end of all things! Likewise, two certain cherubs' heads, from which an ox might learn what true beauty is; and if the 'Presentation of Mary', and the woman selling eggs underneath, do not please you, then call me a blockhead! Think of Goethe when you see the Lions in front of the Arsenal: *Stehen zwei altgriechische Löwen*[8] etc. Sail in a gondola at night, meeting other black gondolas hurrying along. If you don't then think of all sorts of love stories, and other things which might occur within them while they glide by so quickly, then I am a dolt!

Florence – The following are among my notes on the portrait gallery (see if you find them true, and write to me on the subject) –

'Comparison between the head and its production, between the man's work and his exterior – the artist and his portrait. Titian, vigorous and royal; Domenichino, precise, bright, very astute and buoyant; Guido, pale, dignified, masterly, keen; Lanfranco, a grotesque mask; Leonello Spada, a good-natured *fanfaron*[9] and a reveller; Annibale Carracci, peeping and prying; the two Carraccis, like the members of a guild; Caravaggio, rather commonplace and cat-like; Guercino, handsome and affected, melancholy and dark; Bellini the red-haired, the stern, old-fashioned teacher; Giorgione, chivalrous, fantastic, serene and clear; Leonardo da Vinci, the lion; in the middle, the fragile, heavenly Raphael, and over him, Michelangelo, ugly, vigorous, malignant; Carlo Dolce, a coxcomb; Gerard Dow, a mere appendage among his kitchen utensils,' etc, etc.

In the large gallery to the left of the tribune, look at a little picture by Fra Bartolommeo, scarcely larger than this piece of paper, but with two doors, all so neatly and carefully painted and finished. When you enter the gallery, salute first the busts of the Medici, for they were its founders. In the tribune there are some good things. Do not fail to see all the painted churches, which are quite beyond belief – Maria Novella, St Annunziata (you must see Andrea del Sarto there; remember also Fra Bartolommeo falling backwards downstairs from terror, because the angel has already been painting the canvas). Examine also this said angel's painting of the 'Annunciation'[10] of Fra Bartolommeo; it is very fine (Hensel laughs).

To St Marco, the Academy, etc, etc.

If the site of Brunelli's statue, near the Duomo, does not please you, I can't help you. The Duomo itself is not bad. Walk about a great deal.

Milan – Don't fail to go to the top of the cathedral, on account of the millions of pinnacles and the splendid view.

Genoa – It is pleasant to be in the Villetta Negri[11] at nightfall.

Betwixt Genoa and Florence – See everything. Do not miss visiting the Church of St Francesco in Assisi, on any account whatever. The same with regard to all of Perugia.

Drink a flask of *aleatica*[12] in Florence and add another of *vino santo*.

Rome – Holy Week; be as weary as you please during the whole chanting of the Psalms, it's no matter, but listen carefully when they intone the last 'Benedictus Dominus Israel' – all four voices *unison fortissimo* in D minor – it sounds very grand. Observe the strange modulations produced by chance, when one unmusical priest after another takes the book and sings; the one finishing in D major and the other commencing in B flat minor. Above all, see and hear everything in the Sistine Chapel, and write some melodies, or something, from thence to your F. M. B. Greet old Santini.[13] Feast your eyes on the brilliant aspect of the chapel on Palm Sunday, when all the cardinals are robed and carry palms, and when the procession with the singers arrives. The 'Improperia' on Good Friday, in B flat major, are very fine. Notice when the old cardinal sings the 'Credo', the first day of Easter, and all the bells ring out, and the ceremony becomes alive once more, with canon shots, etc, etc. Drive to the *Grotta ferrata*, it is really quite too lovely, and all painted by Domenichino. Don't forget the echo near Cecilia Metella. The tower stands to the left of the road. In the same direction, about fifty yards further, among some old ruined walls and stones, there is the most perfect echo I ever chanced to meet with in my life; it seems as if it never would cease muttering and murmuring. It begins in a slight degree, close behind the tower, but the further you proceed, the more mystical it becomes. You must try to find the right spot. Learn to distinguish between the different orders of monks.

Naples – When there is a storm at Chiatamone, and the grey sea is foaming, think of me. Don't fail to live close to the sea. I lived in Santi Combi, Santa Lucia (I think No. 13), it was most lovely there. Be sure you go from Castellamare to Amalfi, *over* Mount St Angelo. It is the chief highway of all Italy. Proceed from Amalfi to Atrani, and see the church there, and then view the whole glorious landscape from above. Never get overheated. And never fly into a passion. And never be so delighted as to agitate yourself. Be wonderfully haughty and arrogant; all the beauty is there for you only.

Eat as a salad, broccoli with ham, and write to me if it is not capital. So far, my good advice. Enough for today. Farewell, dearest Fanny and dear Hensel family all. We think of you daily and hourly, and rejoice in our good fortune and in your enjoyment.

Felix

The Amalfi Coast, 1831, by Felix Mendelssohn. Felix wrote to his sister of the 'glorious landscape' of the area.

Italy was a great education for Fanny and Felix alike, on top of their striking knowledge of Classical antiquity; both siblings had a wide appreciation of matters artistic and intellectual. Fanny's reply to Felix's letter (also September 1839) is both plentiful and full of opinions. Their like-mindedness gives the impression they could almost be talking together in the same room. Naturally, when the music-making starts, in November 1839, it is included in her account. However, her opinion of the standard of singing in the Sistine Chapel speaks volumes. There's a rather charming piece of gossip with her sister Rebecka about the dull company and lack of balls (dances). Her appreciation of the out-of-the-way Campo Vaccino shows she is not just taken up with the famous places. But the final insult was being woken by the crude sounds of the country pipers.

From Fanny to Felix: Munich, 23 September 1839

Before our departure tomorrow, I must thank you again for your nice recipe for an Italian journey, dearest Felix. I will make every attempt to follow it. With regard to the portrait gallery in Florence, I've only read your observations once because I intend to make my own and then compare them with yours. But there are a few that made such a deep impression on me because of their obvious truth that I'll probably jot them down. For who will dispute that Raphael is a master and Carlo Dolci a fool?

I've remembered your favourites in the Pinakothek and gone to see them, but you wouldn't recognise them in their present form. There can scarcely be any place more splendid than the two rooms housing 95 paintings by Rubens. One has to stand in awe of this monumental talent. Do you remember the portrait of Frau von Vandyk with her child? The woman looks so noble and fine and slightly sad, and even a tiny bit boring. And what about his portrait of an Antwerp organist? That is an extremely good likeness of all tenors, for one can imagine him singing 'Dies Bildnis ist bezaubernd schön' in reference to himself.[14] And the young blond Vandyk is quite good too. Munich is an interesting city. We've been here two weeks and only scratched the surface. We could easily use twice as much time, because what is happening here in new art and the acquisition of art is very significant and meaningful on the highest level. Glass painting, fresco technique, encaustic painting, architecture, carved and cast sculpture, and porcelain are all new and important in their own right.

You can imagine how much my husband has enjoyed seeing so many ideas in his field, as well as artists he's known since his days in Rome.[15] I knew no one here and therefore my head was stuffed full of new things and new people. It's always heartening to discover that people who are away from home are welcome and treated with great hospitality. We've only made a cursory visit to the Glyptothek. But autumn impels us over the mountains and we're planning to make the highest mountain journey in the express coach; we want to go over the Stelvio Ridge. You know that I've had the burning desire to see such a Pass since I was young, and now I'm to have my chance. My husband will thereby become acquainted with an entirely new section of Italy. I hope we'll be away from the very severe Munich autumn air in five or six days and then pass into spring. We'll journey over the lakes into Milan, and if we encounter nice weather, the trip will be particularly magnificent. If either of you writes to Berlin soon, please tell them that they shouldn't worry if they don't hear from us for a while. It will be about a week before we'll be able to write, and since we're starting out with very full travelling days, the letter will take even longer. It's a peculiar feeling, however, to leave the fatherland by going over the Alps, but it must be a similar feeling when travelling by sea. On the other hand, a flat, arbitrary border is nothing. Adieu, dear Felix and Cécile! Your Fanny

Fanny's tour of Italy included the enjoyment of much art, and a good deal of music-making. Meeting the young Prix de Rome artists at the Académie Française changed Fanny's life, both through the performing opportunities it gave and by the appreciation she received. Being fêted by artists such as Jean-Auguste-Dominique Ingres and Charles Gounod gave her a new confidence. She was much impressed with the treasures and gardens of the Vatican.

From Fanny to Felix: Rome, 29 November 1839

This is our fourth day in Rome, and – I am almost ashamed to confess it – I have hardly seen anything yet. The weather is bad, and my husband has so far been running about the whole day long. I wish you could see him: it is quite delightful to see his eyes beaming with happiness. He has met with the very kindest reception; everybody seems to be so glad to see him again, and all ask after Grahl;[16] indeed the whole thing amuses me greatly. His reputation and Felix's have smoothed my path wonderfully, but I feel oppressed with the responsibility of doing honour to my relatives.

Meantime, here is December 2, and I have had to make my *début* (without an instrument to practise on at home) at a musical soirée like our Sunday-music – but at whose house, do you think? Cavaliere Landsberg's.[17] He lets instruments out on hire at ten scudi a month, but for old friendship's sake offered me one at nine, which I declined. He is quite an important personage here, and has a pretty *salon*, with a splendid instrument; he receives ladies and gentlemen with grace, *ma non troppo*, accompanied a small tenor in 'Adelaide', and induced another lady to play two trios and me one, while Madame Vanutelli, a beautiful lady with pleasant manners, played the part of listener.

All this while I couldn't help thinking of Rietz and David making him believe that Cerf was going to send him to prison for playing at our house on a Sunday, and of that other day when Spitzeder painted his face like a herald. Verily times have changed him! Our first visitor in Rome was L., and I must tell you the best thing he said. I played a piece, after which he made the following remark in his Berlin dialect: 'The theme of that piece reminds me very much of an Italian Air that I cannot remember. Don't you know Hensel?'

Yesterday we were at the Sistine Chapel, and I saw the pope and all the cardinals very well, as they passed by . . . Women, unfortunately, are placed in a section behind a grill from which they cannot see anything . . . though we are obliged to sit still for three hours, listening to the *incorrect* and indifferent singing of the pope's choir, and to the not very interesting performance of Mass by a few cardinals, with quavering voices. Still, I shall go there often, for it will be better as one gets accustomed to it, and it is one of these duties one's conscience enjoins upon a traveller.

Picture my distress, dear Rebecka. The Ambassadors are not going to give any balls this year. And I should so have liked to dance a gallop with Kestner.[18] Altogether the season is very dull, Rome is empty, the whole world has gone to Naples, and the rest are left lamenting. However, I do not mind it at all. But I cannot understand why St Ursula does not bring her 11,000 virgins to Rome, for this one week I have made the acquaintance of 12,000 bachelors, and there may be more whom I do not know. Children, too, are rare here, much more so than antiquities. However, I discovered today a boy of eight, who will probably have Italian and French lessons with Sebastian.

But how beautiful the Campo Vaccino is! This, again, is one of those out-of-the-way places that surprise one, in spite of all the pictures and descriptions one may have seen or read; not that it is exactly striking, and the effect it produces is not so much extravagant as peculiar. It keeps on increasing, though, and, as one may say, it bides its time. St Peter's, on the other hand, asserts itself at once, the building and its surroundings are in such complete harmony. It has the air of wishing all beholders to say 'How beautiful though art!' and it is impossible to help saying so. Although conscious of this desire to impress, one is not offended at it, so overpowering is the effect, and so immediate. The Campo Vaccino, on the other hand, has so much of accident about it. Nature and time have converted the imposing buildings of the Romans into a heap of ruins, the charm of which, however, is unparalleled. They are now digging away, and bringing to light pillars, walls, and tessellated pavements, but there is still much buried, and the green grass is fast covering what has been so lately exposed; the part above the ground, however, remains a silent observer of this age, as it has been of so many before it.

Good-bye! It is just striking eleven, and regularly at six in the morning the *pifferari*[19] rouse me from my slumbers. Theirs is the most horrid music ever produced by human lungs and goat's hide, and can indeed only be outdone by the playing of the Italian organists. No one who has not heard it would believe what that is like; to me the priest singing Mass is the divinest music because it silences the organ. Good-bye dearest family! I would gladly refuse an invitation from L. to spend an evening with you.
Fanny

A few years at the Académie Française, at the Villa Medici in Rome, was the prize for select French artists for the purpose of studying art and architecture; home to numerous French artists developing creative projects, they were known as *pensionnaires*.

From Fanny to the Family: Rome, 8 December 1839

Yesterday we dined for the first time with Ingres, director of the French Academy, who received us most kindly. He retains an affectionate remembrance of Paul, whom, to distinguish from Felix, he always calls *Votre frère qui joue si bien de la basse.*[20] As you know he [Ingres] is a great

The Académie Française at the Villa Medici, Rome, where the Hensels dined with Ingres and young French scholars in residence. Painting by Francis Marius Granet, 1807–08.

fiddler before the Lord, and after dinner we had Trios, as is the case every Sunday. The whole French Academy were assembled, all looking thoroughly *jeune France*, with beards and hair *à la Raphael*, and nearly all handsome young men, whom I could not blame for longing after the flesh-pots of Egypt, in the shape of the balls Horace Vernet used to give. There is no dancing to Ingres's fiddle, for he will have nothing but ultra-classical music. You may think of us there now and then, on a Sunday evening. I thought much of Felix in that house, as you may fancy.

A grand institution is this French Academy, and how well off the French artists are together! The gifted engraver Calamatta[21] is constantly at work for Ingres, engraving even his portraits, which is what I call being thoroughly well-to-do in the world. Then how beautiful this Villa Medici is, and what an enviable post is that of Director here at Rome, the very centre of the art-world, with enormous powers of influence over the pick of the young artists in his own country. It is impossible to imagine a more delightful position for an artist; but, unfortunately, people get spoiled, and do not know when they are well off. I am sure most of us are the better for roughing it a little.

Rome, 11 December 1839

Today is Father's birthday, and at Berlin the shops are beginning their Christmas display. Here we are enjoying bright sunshine, and have let out our fire, which, so far, we have only wanted morning and evening.

This week I beheld for the first time the priceless treasures of the Vatican, and also, what few strangers are allowed to see, the private apartments of the pope.[22] This tough old man of seventy-five has had all his rooms newly furnished, in good but simple taste – red damask, with green curtains – as if he means to occupy them for years to come. We admired his splendid ivory crucifixes and inlaid chairs, but the best of all was the view, with the Albanian hills, Monte Cavo, the Campo Annibale, and Frascati in the distance, Rome in the foreground, and the Piazza of St Peter's at our feet.

Then we went to see the museum; the *Stanze*[23] are mostly in excellent condition, especially that of Heliodorus. The *Mass of Bolsena*[24] is wonderful – indeed, so is everything! In *one* room are the Transfiguration, the Madonna di Foligno, the Coronation of St Mary, and the Communion of St Jerome. The Transfiguration, of course, was doubly interesting to me; the copy is really excellent. The servants in the gallery were so delighted to see Wilhelm again, it was quite touching, especially Rinaldi, who used to wait on him.

We merely passed through the sculpture galleries, and went on to the gardens. The first, which stands pretty high, is full of flower-beds, and contains the bronze fir-cone from the Castel S. Angelo. Thence we went to a second garden on undulating ground, with enormous orange trees on espaliers, and hedges of roses and myrtle. On the left you have a view of the Dome of St Peter's, and on the right, of Monte Mario and the Villa Mellini. There is a summer house containing some pretty old sculptures, majolica floors, etc, and all about are fountains, ponds – where the pope feeds the fish – animals of different kinds, and all sorts of beautiful and interesting objects. The views, too, are very varied, from the unevenness of the ground. They presented us with some of the pope's oranges, which are ripening in our rooms. The grapes are still excellent, but neither the pears nor the bread are half as good as they were in Venice.

The Mendelssohn family normally celebrated birthdays and special holidays together, so Fanny is missed at New Year 1839/1840. The first paragraph in the following letter illustrates how much Felix appreciated Fanny's compositions; then follows a delightful play on how busy he has been. The absurd question of her knowing 'all the cardinals' indicates the detail expected of their observations. Then there is more advice, and the letter ends with characteristic affection.

From Felix to Fanny: Leipzig, 4 January 1840

This little page shall go to Rome from here,
And wish you prettily a good new year.

You see my letter begins in true ballad-monger style; if you chance to be in the Colosseum at the moment you receive it, the contrast will be rather grotesque. Whereabouts do you live in Rome? Have you eaten broccoli and ham? Or *zuppa Inglese*?[25] Is the convent of San Giovanni et Paolo still standing? And does the sun shine every morning on your buttered roll? I have just played to Ferdinand Hiller[26] your Caprices in B flat major, G major, E major and F major, which surprised us both; and though we tried hard to detect the cloven hoof in them, we could not do so – all was unmixed delight.

Then I vowed at last to break through my obstinate silence. Pray forgive it! It happened thus: first came the christening, and with it, my Mother and Paul. In the meantime the subscription concerts had begun; then my Mother left us; then Paul, a fortnight later; then came Hiller to stay with us, intending to remain a week, heard a couple of rehearsals and decided to remain the whole winter, for the purpose of completing his oratorio of 'Jeremiah',[27] and producing it here in March; then came an abominable cold and catarrh, which for three weeks confined me to bed, or to my room; then came Breitkopf and Härtel, begging to have the manuscript of my second set of four-part songs, which they have now got, and the trio, which they have not yet got; then came the copyist, petitioning for the score of the new Psalm, which was performed most gloriously the day before yesterday, as a commencement to the new year's concert; then came 116 friends; then came Madame Pleyel,[28] who counts for 216 more and she played the piano right well; then came Christmas, to which I was forced to contribute fourteen gifts, some musical, some pictorial, some practical and some juvenile; and now comes the benefit concert of Mademoiselle Meerti, so here you have an *abrégé* of my *histoire universelle* since my last letter.

But tell me, for Heaven's sake, what are you doing at Rome? 'The finest part of the *old hole* is its situation' said General Lepel[29] once; but he is mistaken. There are still greater charms within her walls. What do you say, bye the bye, to the drone of the *pifferari*, whom the painters paint so admirably,[30] and which produce such indescribable sensations in every nose, while sounding through it? – and to the church music of St Luigi dei

Francesi and others? I should like to hear you on that subject. Can you tell me the names of all the cardinals from a mere glimpse of their hoods or trains? I could do this. When you are with a certain *Madame* by Titian in the Sciarra Palace and with two other certain *Mesdames* also by him (the one in a state of nature, the other unfortunately not) in the Borghese Palace, or with the 'Galatea', or any other Raphael, if you do not then think of me, and wish I were in Rome, I shall assuredly in that case wish you were the Marchesa Muti Papazurri,[31] whose breadth is greater than her height, and that is five feet six inches.

I will now give you some advice. Go to Monte Testaccio and settle yourself comfortably in one of the little inns there; you will feel precisely the same as if you were in Rome. If you have already seen Guido's *Aurora*[32] be sure you go to see it again. Mark well the horrible fifths of the papal singers when they adorn each of their four parts at the same moment with flourishes. On a fine Sunday, go on walking the whole day, till the sun sets, and it becomes cool; then come down from Monte Pincio, or wherever you may be, and have your dinner. Compose a vast deal, for it gets on famously in Rome. Write me soon a long letter. Look out of the window of any convent near the Lateran, towards the Albano mountains. Count the houses in Frascati in the sunshine; it is far more beautiful there than in all Prussia and Poland too.

Forgive this hare-brained letter, for I could not make it better. Farewell, dearest Fanny. May God bless you and your journey and your whole year; and continue to love your – Felix

Fanny's next letter (25 February 1840) gives full accounts of the many joys they have experienced at the Carnival, including the wild behaviour, the elaborate costumes, the colourful carriages and people, the crazy horse race, the day of the *moccoletti* (when the revellers carry lighted candles) and the different ways of engaging with the antics. She contrasts the excitable and expressive Italians with her own more sober-minded northern manner; and her uncharacteristic behaviour (participating in the exuberance) provokes her to ask her mother if she is recognisable!

From Fanny to the Family: Rome, 25 February 1840

We are still in the full tide of the merry Carnival, and I am far more amused with it all than I expected. I need not enter on a formal description, for Goethe took that trouble off my hands fifty years ago, and not only the principal features, but even many of the masks, have remained unaltered since then. The chief day, that of the Mocoletti, is still to come.

We have tried all modes of seeing the fun, from a balcony in the Corso (in three different situations), walking, and driving in a carriage, and I decidedly prefer the last. In this manner you are carried safely and comfortably through the crowd, and also get the best of the fun, which consists in the war maintained against the carriages from the houses, and also by the two rows of carriages between themselves. The different missiles, *confetti* (made of plaster of Paris), sugar-plums large and small, and bouquets, the latter being, of course, the most *distingué*, are generally returned in kind, and Sebastian was quite indignant with me the other day for sending a bouquet in reply to a volley of *confetti*, because I happened to have nothing else at hand. Flour is *mauvais genre*, and, properly speaking, forbidden, but bushels of it are used notwithstanding. Altogether a good many people, especially strangers, treat the whole thing without any grace, and find their amusement in the quantity and hardness of the materials, which they shower down from a safe distance in the second or third storey. Even from quite near, you get very sharp volleys in the face; but everyone is mad enough or sensible enough to take no offence, but try and revenge themselves in the best way possible. The Prince of Syracuse,[33] brother of the King of Naples, hired a balcony, and poured down such an inexhaustible stream of flour that it was hardly possible to pass his corner; but a young Roman noble who had specially suffered from his pelting had *confetti* made in the shape of macaroni, and *riposted* with them the next day, which they say so annoyed the Neapolitan macaroni-eater that he has been better behaved ever since.

Among the most amusing of the caricatures was a gaily decorated cart, containing a body of surgeons armed with huge forceps in which they held skulls, and teeth, singly and in sets, a tremendous squirt, and other instruments of torture, all on the most gigantic scale. On the box was a man who had been trepanned, and at the back sat a savage. In this manner they paraded the Corso, shouting out panegyrics on their own skill, till at last they stopped in front of a balcony, on which sat a bevy of ladies, and, having held a consultation as to their health, they declared unanimously that all the symptoms indicated the use of the syringe, raised their squirt, and ejected from it – a large bouquet. A fellow with a big beard, in a woman's gown and cap, but without a mask, went stumbling about complaining that he could not find a place to be brought to bed in. Many of the coachmen are dressed up as women, and in some cases are by no means bad-looking.

The large carriages, gaily decorated and with wheels wreathed with laurel, are very pretty. They generally carry about a dozen maskers dressed precisely alike, which have an irresistible comic effect; but when you see one of these carriages coming, you must look out for your face, as you are sure to receive a perfect hail of *confetti*. Most ladies wear wire-masks for protection, but I can only have a veil, as I cannot do without my glasses. On the Giovedi Grasso,[34] one of the best days, I drove out with a daughter of

Thorwaldsen, a very pleasant woman, and her niece, and Sebastian. You cannot imagine how fully one is occupied on these occasions. What with keeping one's eyes open to see the fun and avoid being pelted – what with returning, if possible with interest, the fire one has received, and arranging the ammunition collected in the carriage – what with keeping up a conversation with the masks who climb on the step, and behave like acquaintances till they can find an opportunity of throwing something in your face, I can assure you one's hands are full. However, one gets into the spirit of it, and before long feels almost insulted if a carriage passes without throwing, it looks so like neglect.

Do you recognise your daughter, dear mother, frolicking away for hours in the midst of this turmoil, and in a noise which can be compared neither to the roaring of the sea nor to the howling of wild beasts, being like nothing but itself? I believe the open air has a great deal to do with it, for in a room it would be intolerable.

I shall never forget one of the masks I saw yesterday – a tall, thin, young man dressed as a *ci-devant jeune homme*, in a scarlet silk coat, with swallow-tails trailing on the ground. The so-called *Conti*, too, with paper collars three yards long, and wigs of mixed red and yellow curls, look very nice. The gardeners with their long scissors exist still as Goethe described them, and unfortunately the same accident he mentioned happened a few days ago – five horses started a few minutes late for the race, and, darting through the crowd, which always flows together again the moment after it has been divided, knocked down several people. Two have died already, and the number wounded is from four to twelve, according to different accounts.

Ever since, the guard have been a little stricter, but the soldiers have really a disagreeable duty to perform, for the excited populace only jeer and laugh at them when they want to make room, and will not be kept from running across the road behind their backs. They are just like naughty children, for of course the order has only been given for their own safety. Such mad proceedings in the most sober-minded city in the world really form a remarkable contrast. If we could have anything so amusing in Berlin, the Leipziger Strasse would be a splendid locality for it, much better than the Corso.

Family news was very important to Fanny. Rome was a great distance from home, and she laments hearing so late about the birth of Marie, second child of Felix and Cécile (on 2 October 1839); the news only reached Fanny on 4 March 1840. Her news follows – where they live, what she eats, her opinion of the painting of Madame Titian, and reasons why she could not recognise the cardinals. Two days later there is more criticism of the papal music, the description of the ball for the orphans in Capitol Square lit by torchlight, but

Opposite. Facsimile letter from
Fanny Hensel to Felix (Rome,
4 March 1840).

ruined by rain; despite more bad weather, they clearly loved the carnival,
with its mad, manic atmosphere.

From Fanny to Felix: Rome, 4 March 1840

Dear, dear *pater, peccavi*! It is by no means my fault, however, because
while I was scolding you in my letters to Berlin, the nicest letter was salted
away here at the post office for six – I repeat six – weeks. *Oimé!* My husband
went there often before he got sick even though we were no longer
expecting any letters *poste restante*. Instead, we were expecting your letters
through Valentini. But even then, they must have withheld the letter from
him – the *asinacci!* – which is comparable to our having heard about
Cécile's delivery one week late in Venice. Just recently we gave
Kaselowsky[35] a letter to take to the post office and asked him if he might
casually inquire whether there was any mail for us. And then back he came
with the most marvellous letter. I read it six times in a row and died
laughing over it six-hundred times. But, as you can see, I'm still alive. You
rob me of my health when you don't write more often, because you have
no idea how healthy it is to laugh.

What have I been doing in Rome? Going around by myself the first two
months. We made a respectable *giro* and are still far from finished. I took
care of my husband the third month and thus didn't get any farther than
Monte Pincio, which I often approached in tears because I was *supposed* to
walk and yet was so worried and upset. Then Carnival time arrived, and
since my husband began to regain some of his strength, we took him along
with great pleasure, and I had a better time than I ever thought possible.
Last night we had the *moccoli*[36] ceremony and now it's over. We'll start to
travel around the city once again, because our precious time is
unfortunately coming to an end here, and we still have a great deal to do
before Easter. We are living in the Via del Tritone, which runs into the
Piazza Barbarini. If we turn two corners we arrive at the *passeggiate*[37] to
Monte Pincio, and we often took advantage of the proximity of this
pleasant, sunny walk with its decent view, especially when Hensel was
recovering. I haven't had broccoli salad yet, even though you've told me
twice that I'm obliged to do so. Excuse the oversight. But I've just ordered it
for tomorrow.

My God – I'm crazy about Madame Titian who is hanging in the
Sciarra Palace, and I've been fascinated by her since Florence. There she
was in the Uffizi – unfortunately not in the gallery – under the name
Flora,[38] with a white blouse and a handful of flowers, looking as much like a
goddess as a scamp. She can also be seen in the Barbarini Palace sporting a
wig, *à la* Bellini, a dress completely sprinkled with colour (my husband says
it was painted with his blood), a thick hanging chain (my husband says it

Rom, 4ten März, 1840.

Lieben, lieber Peter, peccavi! aber es ist durchaus nicht meine Schuld, wenn während ich dich eben darüber schelten ließ, lag, ohne hier auf der Post steckt, sage sechs Wochen lang, der schönste Brief eingepöckelt! seit zu seiner Krankheit ging mein Mann oft hin, obgleich wir schon lange keine postrestante Briefe mehr erwarteten, [...] seit dem Valentini aufzugeben hatten, aber schon damals mußten sie ihn ihm vorenthalten; die assisei, wie in Venedig, wo es keine Postbindung [...] 8 Tage später erfahe, als nöthig. Endlich nun, schickten wir [...] Briefe ihn hin, u. wir baten Sie beiläufig immer [...], u. damit kam der wunderschönste Brief, den ich Dutzendmal für uns einander gelesen, u. nicht sechsundertmal dabei [...] habe, ich glaube aber ich lebe noch. du begehst wesentlich einen Raub an meiner Gesundheit, wenn du mir nicht öfter schreibst, denn du glaubst gar nicht, wie gesund es mir ist, mich bratzen lassen. Meine vorhabtlichen Dinge und dergleichen will ich dir später auseinandersetzen. Was ich in Rom treibe? Nicht zu viel die ersten 2 Monate. wir haben einen ordentlichen Hausstand gemacht, u. sind noch lange nicht fertig. den 3ten Monat meines Herrn [...] er nicht weiter gekommen als monte Pincio, wo ich oft mit grünen Frauen ging, weil ich spazieren gehen sollte? Auch dort so ängstlich und gemütlich. Dann kam Carneval, u. da mein Mann eben wieder anfing etwas vertragen zu können, so haben wir ihn mit [...] Halbiges mitgemacht, u. ich habe mich amüsiert, wie ich nie gedacht hätte. Gestern Abend haben wir moccoli gehabt, u. nun ist das, u. wir werden wieder anfangen uns ein wenig herumzutreiben, denn leider geht die köstliche Zeit auch zu Neige? Ich muß nachholt, gar viel geschehen bis Ostern. Wohnen thun wir in der via del Tritone, die in piazza Barberini ausläuft. Wenn wir um 2 St aufgeh find wir auf der passeggiata auf monte Pincio, und die Nähe dieses sonnigen Spazierganges mit erträglicher Aussicht wird uns schon oft, besonders während Wilhelms Genesungszeit, sehr angenehm. broccoli als Palast habe ich noch immer nicht gesehen, obgleich du es mir schon zweimal sehr höflich gemacht, verzeih diese Nachlässigkeit, ich habe ihn aber eben auch morgen bestellt. Gott, die Wundermadonnen, im Palast Sciarra, liebt ich ja schon entsetzlich seit Florenz, wo sie in den Uffizien, leider nicht in der Tribüne, unter dem Namen Florenz, mit einem einzigen Hunde u. einer Handvoll blumen hängt, [...] eben so viel von einer Göttin als von einem Backersai. [...]

made Titian look her prisoner), and a marvellously fresh face. But the gorgeous little minx looks naughty, and surely must have made his life both wonderful and miserable.

How would I, a nobody, have made the acquaintance of all the cardinals? I'm definitely near-sighted, never get into the Sistine Chapel, and am very far from the holiness of the caps and tails in St Peter's. Therefore, I only see these men when they loosen their tails, and then they look nothing less than beautiful.

I already received a clear impression of papal fifths at Christmas.[39] This is the perpetual refrain: [manuscript of 2 bars of chords]. And if those aren't fifths, then I don't know what fifths are. I've only heard other church music at Sta Maria Maggiore on one occasion, when the *Vera cella* sounded merry. But I've had enough. Out of sisterly love I wanted to hear the nuns at Trinità,[40] but it's very difficult to gain entry now and I would've been forced to hide myself behind one of my devout cousins. The day before yesterday there was a festival here which, in terms of local standards, was probably unique: a ball at the Capitol Square for the benefit of the cholera orphans. One climbed up through the Forum, illuminated with countless torches, and in whose glow the old figures on the columns looked eerie and fantastic. The capitol square itself, with its statues of Marcus Aurelius and the Dioscuri, also looked splendid in the torchlight. Unfortunately, it was pouring cats and dogs, and one can imagine how much more wonderful the place would have looked on a moonlit evening.

In general, the Carnival was not favoured by good weather. The first day we had awful *tramontane*[41] and then rain. Even the *moccoli* evening had to be celebrated with umbrellas, but nonetheless I had a wonderful time. The event is so mad that it truly approaches the poetic: the countless moving lights, the mad merry shrieking, the masked costumes illuminated in numerous ways, the continual assaults that one must try to repel, and the attempts to reignite the torches that have been extinguished. All this is so bewildering that one no longer knows if his head is on straight. The Italians possess a very special virtuosity in their expressions *senza moccolo*, which rings out from all sides if someone has no light or his torch has gone out, for it conjures up the complex images of mockery, astonishment, pity, deepest regret, questioning, and triumph. One can die laughing when one is thus shouted at on all sides. On the other hand, the expression *sia ammazzato*,[42] which Goethe heard, is no longer in vogue.

In the rest of the letter, Fanny expresses regret at being away while Felix's *Psalm* was being performed, and bemoans the lack of a good piano. She also mentions Friedrich August Elsasser, a landscape artist and friend from Berlin from whom Fanny had received a gift of a drawing, and the painter and sculptor Franz Catel.

From Fanny to Felix: Rome, 4 March 1840 (continued)

Hiller's decision to work hard in Leipzig does him honour. Send him my
very best and tell him how sorry we were not to have met him in Milan. But
in general, we've had bad luck with people on this trip. It's really a shame to
spend an entire season in Rome and not meet up with one single person of
distinction. Liszt was here for four months last year – how I would have
loved to hear the Hungarian magnet! Have you ever heard anything more
ludicrous than this boastful tale? Lablache[43] also could have let himself be
heard by me, and I very much fear that he, or rather I, will become
acquainted with everyone else before I become acquainted with him.

Stop! Which Psalm of yours is being performed now? Is it *Kommt, lasst
uns anbeten* or *Als Israel aus Egypten zog?*[44] Just be careful that the
European Congress doesn't think that you intended Abraham to strike at
the Battle of Nisib[45] when he left Egypt. But send me a serious response to
this question, and also to the matter concerning the piano, i.e. should I buy
one from Felix Gross, citizen of Vienna? I don't want one from Graf because
they are too light, and I've just seen a sobering example, in the person of
one Frau Hensel, of how one can become spoiled. The woman has had an
old, light, played-out rattletrap for three months and received another
ordinary Viennese instrument. I heard her yesterday and can assure you
that she cannot continue this way. Should she come to Leipzig soon, you
would see that she can't play any longer. Every new start is *difficult*.

Oh, and composing! I've already complained in a letter to Berlin that
no ideas strike me any more – nothing good and nothing bad. *Dio mio!*
Abraham is getting old. But now I'll switch from your terrain and speak to
Cécile.

Good day my dearest! If I had enough space, I would scold you and
make you blush, for you should write to me often, very often. You know
very well that your letters cheer me and I find them very interesting. I am
thus forced to hear the most darling stories of little Karl[46] in letters from
Berlin. Congratulations on the pianino. When I visit you again, let's make
some gentle music together. That is truly a lovely present! I've also been
given wonderful presents here: a very beautiful oil sketch and a splendid
ink drawing from Elsasser, and a forthcoming painting from Catel. In
addition, we've given many presents ourselves, and you'll probably like the
gifts we're giving you very much. But I hope we'll find you in Berlin, and if
God grants us good health when we meet, our joy will be complete. With
this devout wish, I want to close and ask you to commend us to the
Schuncks[47] and other Leipzig friends. And please, please – write soon. You
have no idea how happy your letters make us. My husband and the little
man send their best.

Your Fanny

On 10 May Fanny writes about how happy she has been in Rome, and is sad that their time there is coming to an end. Her pleasure continues with the good weather and the beauties of nature, and she tries to anticipate the move to Naples optimistically.

Liszt and Marie d'Agoult had spent four months in Rome in 1839, and the musical world there was impressed with him; Fanny rued missing the opportunity to hear him perform. Given the contrast of Liszt's flamboyance and her sensible nature, she is generous in acknowledging Liszt for dedicating his Beethoven symphony arrangements to Ingres. She also imagines the contrast of her and Felix's different performances of J. S. Bach's concerto for three keyboards, being discerning enough about character to know that different people make music in different ways. Her sense of discrimination continues with the people she meets; she knows she is being critical, so Charivari alludes to an old tradition of a mocking serenade. She has been championing Felix's music, to great effect.

From Fanny to Felix: Rome, 10 May 1840

Dearest Felix, thank you for your dear, humorous letter from the 7th April. I much preferred hearing about your journey to Berlin from you than receiving the letter from Berlin, which let me know that you did indeed arrive there without incident. This letter took almost three weeks to arrive, which is almost impossible to believe, and thus I started to become worried. You went to Berlin at just the right time (not for us, of course), because in the light of the fact that the Worringens[48] just left, and considering Beckchen's little condition,[49] we were afraid that it might become a little too quiet at home before we, as fresh arrivals, could bring back some new life and new stories. If only I could predict when we can see each other and where! I've had my eye on Frankfurt, which we will pass through in any case and which you probably won't want to miss either. Of course, I'd prefer if we were to meet in Leipzig, at your house, and then our trip would come full circle and you could give us lodgings again for a few days. I really want to see you and tell you all about our trip. I can't find words to tell you how happy we are here, and how much we like everything. We've extended our stay until the end of the month, and I see with sadness how time is slipping through our fingers. We couldn't tear ourselves away, and even now I become very sad whenever I think of our departure. Fortunately, Naples is ahead of us, and I look forward to it very much. We're now thinking of spending only a very short time in the city itself and of making excursions from Castellamare,[50] as a number of people have advised us. Perhaps there will be some time left for a few seaside resorts.

We've had such marvellous weather for the past few weeks that it's been a joy to be outside and drink in the air. We were very busy making excursions into the Campagna, which I couldn't love more if I were an artist, and recently spent a delightful day at Tivoli. The Alban hills are still ahead of us. These are the mountains I've seen the entire winter in their incredible beauty. I often made detours and scaled heights in order to see them when I hadn't seen them for a few days, and yet I don't feel the urge to go there now.

All in all, I've been in Rome long enough so that my original travel-fever has subsided. I even agree with Zelter – I'm too young to see everything, and only when you've come to that realisation can true enjoyment begin. There are certainly many things I will not have seen when we leave Rome, but I will have visited my favourite spots over and over again and enjoyed them immensely. Three weeks from today we will be in Naples, please God, and undoubtedly will have a wonderful time there as well.

I would have liked to experience Liszt in Leipzig. Here he is talked about to an astonishing degree. He was here for four months last year and became friendly with Ingres and the musicians at the Pension,[51] just as we have, and they always tell me about him. I'm very sorry that I didn't come upon him, as he must have been especially humane here. He didn't give any concerts but only played at his own residence and Ingres', whatever and as much as people requested. He's dedicated two of his arrangements of Beethoven symphonies to Ingres and sent them to him recently. If the wild rain that's poured down almost incessantly since two nights ago would be so kind as to abate, we'll go there tonight and look at the crazy things for myself. Here they are entranced with the way he plays Beethoven symphonies, whereas you seem less taken with it. I'm curious to hear you describe the experience. I'd love to have heard the Bach concerto from you three. Just think, I'm also performing it this week, with a Danish and an Italian woman, both very good pianists. But no doubt there will be considerable difference between the performances. I tell you the French now admire nothing except *Bacque*[52] – it's really too funny. I've had to play the Concerto in D minor at least a dozen times and they're always wild with delight over it.

They're also very appreciative of your music, and one has to give them credit for their attentiveness and their ability to retain so much after only one hearing. You can't expect more than that. Whenever old Santini[53] sees me, he pesters me to have you send him some music. I'll have to give him one of the pieces I brought with me; I can see that he won't let me leave otherwise. But he's a dear old man, by far the most agreeable person among the wealth of boring ones here. Because that is the other side of Rome: the countless unbearably boring people, especially among the official dignitaries, which include the Germans as well. God, what awful people! But quiet – I've promised my husband not to criticise anybody in letters. I won't, however, gag my mouth against verbal expression, and since Beckchen isn't here with us, I must function as both Charivari and Figaro in the guise of a single person. But here I walk around with rose-tinted glasses and thus let many things pass that I wouldn't at home. Perhaps the air has imparted some of its inexhaustible gentleness to me.

In the letter of 11 May 1840, Fanny is a little envious of Hiller getting such a lot of help from Felix. She too wishes to compose an oratorio.[54] Indeed, she would like to publish. Clearly the singing of the Armenian High Mass was awful, and the papal singers again lost pitch. In softer vein, she anticipates the idea of meeting Hiller at Lake Como, and jests with Cécile.

From Fanny to Felix: 11 May 1840

The rain eased up yesterday, so we went to the Academy and I viewed the Liszt-Beethoven-Ingres symphonies.[55] It's very good that he states in the preface that he wishes to help popularise the works through this edition. If the musical populace or rabble would ever play that, then string me up! For all their technical apparatus, I don't doubt for one moment that you could play them ten times more beautifully.

Congratulations on the success of Hiller's oratorio. If you ever worked that hard with me some time, I would also compose one. I'm truly sorry that I won't be able to experience the celebration of printing somewhere in Germany. That will be a beautiful celebration if ever there was one, and I'd be intrigued to see the actual printing done in the street. I'd love to see how the monks here would celebrate such an occasion: with a Requiem, no doubt.

Have you ever heard an Armenian High Mass? It's the most awful caterwauling that I've ever heard, and meow is the only word that could be clearly understood. The people, of all things, have such beautiful, earnest heads, and the Bishop is such an honourable old man, that one doesn't know whether one should be surprised or feel sorry for these people who grunt at their God in such a cannibalistic manner. The Greeks, on the other hand, sing very well. They have three-part men's choirs, and decently-composed music with a pure, strong, self-assured style of performance that is firmer by far than the papal singers, who began the *Miserere* in B minor both times and ended in G minor once and F minor the other time. We'll also have to discuss that at length. If Spontini[56] hadn't already made suggestions for the improvement of church music, I'd submit a report to His Holiness, for an improvement really is necessary. And since Magnus, the heretic, is painting a cardinal, one can't really tell for sure.[57] I hear that Otto Nicolai was planning to become the director of the papal chapel, and even willing to become a Catholic and a priest – necessary conditions for

the position – since it didn't matter to him. But since the plan failed, he's thrown himself into the arms of opera and is now in Turin.

If Hiller returns to Lake Como in June, it's quite possible that we'll see him there in July. We were at Lake Como only one day, a rainy day at that. It's so heavenly beautiful there that we might well go from Milan to the town of Como, a place we haven't seen yet, if things work out. It's absolutely impossible, however, to see everything in *one* trip to Italy, even if you criss-cross about as much as we did. We'll probably have to give up Parma and Perugia as well, places my husband has never visited. It's too *fatiguant* to travel through all of Italy in the middle of summer – it took six days alone from Rome to Florence – and therefore, if Sebastian and I can endure it, we'll board a steamship from Naples to Livorno.

Dear little Cécile, many thanks for your dear note from Berlin. They write me such dreadful things about you, and you're reputed to look so ugly now,[58] that I'm downright impatient to see you so that I can ascertain whether all that is true. Furthermore, no one at home can stand your children and that must have been particularly unpleasant for you. In my absence little Carl has developed his talent for singing and undoubtedly is a

A view of Lake Como (Cadenabbia), by Felix Mendelssohn. The day the Hensels were there, 22 July 1837, on their honeymoon, was marred by rain.

sweet little charmer by now. I'm very eager to meet my first niece.

What kind of children will there be in Berlin this year? Every letter I've received has given notice of new hopes, and next year something will be crawling and wobbling wherever you look. Farewell for now, dearest people! I do so hope that snow won't fall before we see each other again. After this trip I need it more urgently than ever. My husband sends his best. He's busy with preliminary sketches and is bringing back a few very beautiful heads. We're all well now, thank God, and I'm enjoying my life ever so much. You know, dear Felix, how crazy I am about fresh air, and therefore you can appreciate how happy I am to drink in all this heavenly air. The weather has cleared up after a few rainy days, and we can look forward to the most glorious weather once again. For us now it's a time in which every moment is experienced to the utmost, and every hour has a pulse that one can feel. It's the same for me when we're together with you dear ones. May it happen again soon! Your Fanny

In his letter of 24 October, Felix contrasts the pleasures of travel with the pride he feels about all things German; he compares the annoying demands of the Leipzig *Liedertafel* (song recital series), with the contented quiet of home. His sixth visit to England took place the previous month, with the Birmingham performance of his *Hymn of Praise* on 23 September 1838 receiving great acclaim. He then returned to London, where he visited old friends, including staying with Ignaz and Charlotte Moscheles.

Felix's reference to 'peace or war' was about the uncertainty felt when King Frederick William III of Prussia died in Berlin on 7 June 1840. He had ruled since 1797, through the difficult times of the Napoleonic wars and he had made some token reforms granting Jewish civil equality. At the Congress of Vienna in 1815 his ministers had secured some territorial increases for Prussia.

From Felix to Fanny: Leipzig, 24 October 1840

Dear Fanny,

I make use of my first morning's leisure since my return from England, to thank you for your most admirable and charming letter, which welcomed me on my return here. When I first saw it lying, and broke the seal, I had somehow a kind of presentiment that it might contain some bad news (I mean, something momentous). I don't know how this was, but the very first lines made me see it in a different light, and I read on and on with the greatest delight. What a pleasure it is to receive such a letter, with such a flavour of life and joy, and all that is good! The only tone in a minor key is that you do not expect to like Berlin much after Rome; but this I consider a very transitory feeling; after a long sojourn in Italy, where could anyone be contented? There, all is so glowing and our dear German home life, which I do so heartily love, has this in common with all that is German and dear, that it is neither splendid nor brilliant, but its stillness and repose only the more surely fascinate the heart. After every absence I felt just the same when the joy of the first days of reunion were past; I missed the variety and the excitement of travel so much that home seemed monotonous, and I discovered all sorts of deficiencies, whereas during my journey all was perfect, all was good.

The same feelings have often recurred to me recently at the Leipzig *Liedertafel*, and at the innumerable demands and intrusions, etc, etc; but this did not last, and was certainly only a fallacy. All that is good, and that we like in our travels, is, in fact, our wonted property at home, only we there exact a still larger portion. If we could only preserve through life the fresh, contented, and lofty tone of feeling which, for the first few days on returning from a journey, leads us to look at every object with such satisfaction, and on the journey makes us rise superior to all annoyances; if we could only remain inwardly in this buoyant travelling spirit, while continuing to live in the quiet of home, we should indeed be vastly perfect! Instead of this, last night, at the twenty-fifth anniversary of the *Liedertafel*, I was as angry as if I had been a young boy. They sang so false, and talked even more falsely; and when it became particularly tiresome, it was in the name of 'our German Fatherland' or 'in the good old German fashion'. Yet, when I came back from England I had formed such a strong resolution never to trouble myself about anything, and to remain entirely neutral! I was eight days in London, and the same in Birmingham, and to me the period passed like a troubled dream; but nothing could be more gratifying than meeting with so many friends quite unchanged. Although I could only see them for so short a time, yet the glimpse into so friendly an existence, of which we hear nothing for years, but which remains so linked with our own, and will ever continue to be so, causes most pleasurable sensations.

Of course I was constantly with Klingemann and Moscheles, and with the Alexanders[59] also, where, in the most elegant rococo drawing-rooms, among all the newest and most fashionable objects, I found my father's portrait, painted by Hensel, in its old favourite place, and standing on its own little table; and I was with the Horsleys also, and in many other houses where I felt happy and at home; when I recall my excessive uneasiness at the prospect of the journey, and how we paced up and down here together and discussed it, making each other, in fact, only more nervous, and yet all is now so happily over, and I so happily returned to my family – I ought scarcely to do anything all day long but rejoice and be thankful – instead of which I fly into a passion with the *Liedertafel*, and you do the same with the Art Exhibition!

You ask me whether we are to have peace or war? How have I got such a

The Bay of Naples, with Vesuvius, by Felix Mendelssohn, 1831, from a book for his son, Paul. Fanny described Vesuvius as 'Satan's headquarters'.

fine reputation as a news monger? Not that I do not deserve it, for I maintain through thick and thin that we shall have peace, but combined with much warlike agitation; though when a *politicus* by profession like Paul is in the family, he must be applied to. He may say what he likes, but no war shall we have.

Pray write again soon, my very dear sister, and a long letter.
Your Felix

On the next phase of their journey, Fanny and Wilhelm arrived in Naples in early June 1840. She was delighted by the richness of nature in the south, and her lovely apartment had a wonderful view of the Bay, which included three English men-of-war. On a visit to the Arts Museum, she unexpectedly met the singer Pauline Garcia, company she relished. The next day, there

were more Italian festivities, with ornamented carriages, bedecked people, exuberant music and choking dust. Her description of their visit to Vesuvius ('Satan's headquarters'), the sulphurous smells and her relief at returning home, all give a strong flavour of how challenging that excursion was. After visiting Vesuvius, she was rather overawed by Pompeii, and the damage wrought by the eruption of AD 79.

From Fanny to the Family: Whit Monday, 8 June

Today the festival of the Madonna dell'Arco took place. We drove seven miles into the country to see it, through an indescribable turmoil the whole way. There were hundreds of vehicles, ornamented with green boughs, handkerchiefs, and ribbons, the people in them carrying sticks like forks, from which were suspended feathers, flowers, saints' pictures, baskets, spoons, and a thousand other articles, purchased at the fair near the church. Everybody was dressed in their best, and there was a running accompaniment of tambourines and castanets, singing and shouting, all seasoned with the choking dust. Near the church the noise was deafening and the crowd enormous; people were sitting in booths drinking, but I saw no excess. Many of the physiognomies and complexions were quite African; one girl especially, who was beating a tambourine and laughing, looked a perfect savage. Wilhelm walked about sketching. We agreed that this festival would form a most appropriate subject for a frieze, as it really does resemble a bacchanalian procession.

I stayed at home in the evening and read some French newspapers full of discussions about the removal of Napoleon's ashes.[60] Stepping out on the balcony afterwards into the moonlight, with the lights on the ships and all around, while nature seemed hushed to repose, I felt a disgust of newspapers such as I had never experienced before.

Last week we made grand excursions to Ischia and Vesuvius. On Sunday we took the steamer to Ischia, a delightful sail. The Bishop's Palace on Procida stands on a little promontory and the town has an almost oriental appearance. The costume of the women resembles that of the modern Greeks. On our arrival at Ischia we were tormented by a double set of people touting, consisting of half the population and all the donkeys, howling, shouting, and fighting for the honour of conveying us to land. We stepped out of the boat onto the donkeys' backs and so rode out of the sea and straight on. The rocks were covered with profuse vegetation, of Indian figs, aloes, pomegranates and vines.

A day's rest set me right and fit for our excursion to Vesuvius, which we had carefully planned for Sebastian's birthday. After the fertile and beautiful pomegranates, oranges and figs, we reached the lava, riding over that of last year, which overwhelmed so many vineyards and left traces still visible in the up-rooted trees and blackened ground; it is not yet quite cold. Then followed a bit of most disagreeable road, over stone of the same kind as that which buried Herculaneum. Soon we entered upon the haunted region, our guides pointing out to right and left the different lava-streams which had descended in such and such years. Finally, we found ourselves on the summit of Satan's headquarters, a stony cindery plain, from which you see the smoke rising. The higher cone at this moment (for it is continually changing its shape) was on our left and we did not go up it. We approached the crater with an indescribable feeling of curiosity and gazed into it with amazement and horror. What a diabolic mess! The sulphurous smell, the colours such as you see nowhere else in nature, green, yellow, red, and blue, all poisonous hues, and the ash grey at the bottom of the cauldron, the smoke now thick, now thin, rising from all the crevices, and enveloping everything while it conceals nothing – all this, changing with every step, made up a spectacle of horror.

We climbed up the opposite side of the crater and were rewarded by a prospect of overwhelming beauty – the bay of Naples, the islands, the rocky peaks behind the villages – all this we gazed upon for the first time, with a feeling almost of awe, from that gruesome eminence. Turn round and you see a wide crater. Turn again and there rises a dismal mound of yellow-green sulphur and lava, which realises all one's ideas of the infernal regions. Our difficult retreat began after sunset; I preferred sacrificing my feet to letting them carry me; it is a fearful business. We were quite smothered by the smoke, and kept sinking up to our knees in the ashes, which filled our shoes at every step; we made our way, wading, panting and stumbling. Pitch darkness set in and I was left far behind with my guide; I learned what fear was! It was night when we found our horses, which carried us to the hermitage. We were back in Naples by half-past twelve, and I assure you the sight of houses, carriages, chairs, and last but not least, my bed, was more grateful than I can say.

On Monday morning we rode on donkeys to Pompeii under a thick and lowering sirocco. This is one of those sights which impress one with awe, and, if I may be allowed the expression, with solemn curiosity. None of us could speak except in a low tone. Having seen the crater beforehand, one understands how likely the event was to happen. Vesuvius, like some grim phantom, frowns down upon the silent streets, and nothing can be imagined more awe-inspiring than the aspect of this stern destroyer, still armed with the same power of doing mischief, while at his feet are the speaking witnesses of the horrid wrong-doing he committed eighteen centuries ago. The mounds of small stones and ashes round the excavated houses complete the vivid picture of the dreadful event to such a degree that you feel as if it happened only yesterday, to people with whom you had been personally acquainted.

From Fanny to the Family: Naples, 9 July 1840

If I were to give my best first, I should begin with the view I am at this
moment privileged to enjoy, but I had rather proceed chronologically, on
which Bousquet accompanied us as far as Genzano.[61] At Terracina, the
scenery suddenly becomes beautiful, with palm trees, the sea, and
grotesque rocks up which the town seems to climb. A harbour is being built
besides other things, so this is actually the first town in Italy in which I have
seen any building going on. We continued our journey, delightful with
luxuriant vegetation. At Gaeta the hotel is close to the sea, with a garden
full of orange trees. To the right is the fortress on the rock; to the left, the
lovely promontory shading off towards the horizon in a soft haze. The
foreground consists of cypresses, pines, orange trees and olives growing
down to the water's edge. After leaving Gaeta you get among hedges of
myrtles, aloes, wild roses, and the vines climb to the top of the tallest trees.

View of Terracina, by Eduard
Primavesi, 1837, where Fanny
writes that 'the scenery
suddenly becomes beautiful'.

   We drove right on to Naples and dropped into the best apartments we
have yet had. They consist of a fine *salon* and three bedrooms, with a

pleasant view over Sta Lucia, Pizzi Falcone, and the island of Capri, with a peep at the sea. Adjoining our *salon* is a larger and better-furnished one, with a balcony about sixty feet long and twenty-five wide, belonging to the most amiable of Englishmen, Lord Cavendish, who retains it during his stay at Castellamare, and the Cameriere, being as noble-minded as the nobleman, has placed it entirely at our disposal. The view takes your breath away, for you see that part of the town which is towards Vesuvius, with innumerable villas and villages dotted over its base, the hermitage at the foot of the cone, and the cone itself, looking very uncanny and awful in the midst of the glorious landscape. Just under our feet is a fish-preserve, in which the anchovies for our dinner are caught fresh every day. If this is not enough, turn again to the left and behold the English fleet, three great three-deckers, looking as calm and majestic as if they had only come on purpose to add to the beauty of the scene, whereas they are really here to exercise a slight pressure upon the Neapolitan government on the question of Sicilian sulphur.

This morning I met – whom do you think? – your friend Pauline Garcia, now Madame Viardot.[62] I recognised her at once, and we were both delighted at the meeting. It is a pity she has only a few days longer to stay here, and a still greater pity that we were in Rome together for the last few days without knowing it. For an answer to Mother's questions about why our letters smell of musk, I must refer you to the post office. They may perhaps have lain in the vicinity of some sweet love-letter, for no scents of that kind have come across our threshold, or even greeted our noses.

Fanny and Wilhelm Hensel journeyed home via Genoa, Milan, the St Gotthard Pass and Zurich, and returned to visit Felix in Leipzig in September. The accession to the Prussian throne of Frederick William IV in June 1840 brought the prospect of change, with vague promises of a constitution. The king wished to revitalise the arts in Berlin, recruiting Ludwig Tieck to direct the theatre, and Peter Cornelius to give new impetus to painting and sculpture. However, there were low expectations. Overtures were made to Felix in Leipzig to build up the music, but were inconclusive. There is a pessimistic reference to the king at the end of Fanny's travel diary, of which her concluding words were:

Fanny's travel diary

This is Wednesday, and it is six days since our return. Political events look threatening; the king has given a decided refusal to the request of the states for a constitution; the French are openly preparing for war; everything looks dark, dismal and dreary, even the weather, for it is blowing and raining, and so cold that my fingers are benumbed. I hear too that the king can be expected to do nothing for art. Of the impression made upon me by our return home I will write at some future period, when the present has become the past, and the storm has either passed over our heads or expended its force upon us. I have learnt from experience that there are subjects which it is best not to deal with at the time.

As suggested, Fanny took her time and composed *Das Jahr* a year later.

In February 1841, Felix refers in warm terms to Karl Anton Florian Eckert, who later became *Kapellmeister* of the *Staatsoper Unter den Linden*. More significantly, Felix is vexed at missing Fanny's brilliant Sunday music concerts, and then goes on to make a poor joke about the slow tempo in his Psalm *Sing to the Lord for ever and ever*.

From Felix to Fanny: Leipzig, 14 February 1841

Salut et Fraternité!

Have you read the wrathful letter which the Emperor of China wrote to Lin, with a bright red pencil? Were this the fashion with us, I would write to you today with a grass-green pencil, or with a sky-blue one, or with whatever colour a pleasant pencil ought to assume, in gratitude for your admirable epistle on my birthday.

My especial thanks also for the kind and friendly interest you have shown in the faithful Eckert; he is a sound and practical musician, and further than this, in my opinion (to which I sometimes adhere for twenty-four hours), no man should concern himself about another. Whether a person be anything extraordinary, unique, etc., is entirely a private matter. But in this world, everyone ought to be honest and useful, and he who is not so, must and ought to be abused, from the Lord Chamberlain to the cobbler. Of all the young people whom I have had anything to do with here, he is the most good-natured, and by far the most inoffensive; and these are two precious qualities.

Don't, I beg you, write me anything more about your Sunday Music, it is really a sin and a shame that I have not heard it. But though I feel so provoked at this, it is equally vexatious that you have heard none of our truly brilliant subscription concerts. I tell you we glitter brightly – in Bengal fire.

The other day, in our last historical concert (Beethoven), Herr Schmidt was suddenly taken ill and could not sing his 'Ferne Geliebte' in the 'Liederkreis'. In the first part David said 'I see Madame Devrient.'[63] She had arrived that morning by rail and was to return the next day. So, during an interval, I went up to her, was vastly polite, and she agreed to sing 'Adelaide';[64] on which an old piano was carried into the orchestra from the anteroom. This was greeted with much applause, for people suspected that

Devrient was coming. So, come she did, in a shabby travelling costume, and Leipzig bellowed and shouted without end. She took off her bonnet before the *publicum* and pointed to her black pelisse, as if to apologise for it. I believe they are still applauding! She sang beautifully and there was a great flourish of trumpets in her honour, and the audience clapped their hands, till not a single bow of the shabby pelisse was any longer visible.

As to the *tempi* of my Psalm,[65] all I have to say is that the passage of the Jordan must be kept very watery; it would have a good effect if the chorus were to reel to-and-fro, that people might think they saw the waves; here we have achieved that effect. If you do not know how to take the other *tempi*, ask G—[66] about them. He understands that capitally in my Psalms. With submission, allow me to suggest that the last movement be taken very slow indeed, as it is called 'Sing to the Lord for ever and ever' and ought therefore to last for a very long time! Forgive this dreadful joke.

Adieu dear Fanny

Your Felix

Fanny's life continued in Berlin, notably composing songs and piano pieces, and her most substantial work the *Piano Trio* in D minor, Op. 11. Felix worked hard with the Leipzig Gewandhaus Orchestra and founded the Leipzig Conservatoire in 1843; in 1846 Birmingham commissioned his oratorio *Elijah*.

Dying of a stroke was a recurring event in the Mendelssohn family: Moses, both parents, then Fanny, and then Felix died from apoplexy. As the last letter shows, Felix was completely devastated at the loss of his dearly loved sister; both family health and being broken-hearted meant that he only lived for a further six months. Fanny died on 14 May 1847.

From Felix to Rebecka: Frankfurt, 19 May 1847

Dear Rebecka, God help us all – since yesterday I don't know what else to say and think. I have written to Paul and Hensel, but today and yesterday and for many days to come I shall not know what to write except – God help us, God help us! Yesterday all day long I felt as if I had to travel to Berlin in order to see you and Hensel. *Ach*, if only we had not been apart! It fills me with the most bitter regret. And the only thing that helps even a little is crying quite a lot, if only one could always do so. I cannot write or think of anything but Fanny. What we have all lost, and I above all – that we are not as yet able to measure. With her kindness and love she was part of myself every moment of my life. There was no joy I experienced without thinking of the joy she would feel with me. The wealth of her sisterly love spoiled me and made me proud.

Felix

Das Jahr Epigrams

Each piece of Fanny's *Das Jahr* is preceded by an epigram; there are four by Goethe, two by Uhland, two by Schiller, one by Eichendorff, one ascribed to Tieck and words from a Bach chorale, as well as one by an unknown author. Fanny knew some of these poets personally and the poems add an extra literary dimension to the whole creation. There is a sort of triple counterpoint between the music, artistic and literary elements.

Januar: *Ahnest du, o Seele wieder, Sanfte, süsse Frühlingslieder? Sieh umher die falben Bäume, Ach! es waren holde Träume* (Do you, O soul, sense again Gentle, soft sweet spring songs? Look, everywhere are leafless trees Ah! it was a dream) Ludwig Uhland

Februar: *Denkt nicht, ihr seyd in deutschen Gräntzen Von Teuffels- Narren- und Todtentänzen Ein heitres Fest erwartet euch* (Do not think you are in German lands With the dances of devils, fools and death A merry feast awaits you) Johann von Goethe

März: *Verkündiget ihr dümpfen Glocken schon, Des Osterfestes erste Feyerstunde?* Easter Chorale: *Christ ist erstanden* (Muffled bells already, do you announce the first holiday hour of the Easter celebrations? Easter Chorale: Christ has been created) Goethe

April (Capriccio): *Der Sonnenblick betrüget, Mit mildem falschem Schein* (The glance of the sun betrays itself with its mild traitorous shine) Goethe

Mai: *Nun blüht das fernste, tiefste Thal. Ein Frühlingslied zwischen Sehnsucht und heftiger Leidenschaft . . .* (Spring song, now the distant, deep valley blooms) Uhland

Juni: *Hör' ich Rauschen, Hör' ich Lieder, Hör' ich holde Liebesklage* (Do I hear whispering, Do I hear songs, Do I hear the sweet lament of love?) Unknown

Juli: *Die Fluren dürsten, Nach erquickendem Tau, der Mensch verschmachtet* (The meadows thirst for refreshing dew, the people languish) Friedrich Schiller

August: *Bunt von Farben, Auf den Garben, Liegt der Kranz* (Bright with colours, on the sheaves lies the garland) Schiller

September: *Fliesse, fliesse, lieber Fluss, Nimmer werd ich froh* (By the river, flow, flow, never will I be happy) Goethe

Oktober: *Im wald, im grünen Walde, Da ist ein lustiger Schall* (In the wood, in the green woods, there is a cheerful echo) Joseph Freiherr von Eichendorff

November: *Wie rauschen die Bäume so winterlich schon, Es fliegen die Träume der Liebe davon! . . . Ein Klaglied schallt aus Dämm'rung und Wald* (How the trees rustle so wintery already. They fly away, the dreams of love . . . A lament echoes out of the dusk and forest) Unknown/Tieck (?)

Dezember: *Vom Himmel hoch, da komm ich her* (From heaven above, I come to Earth) Martin Luther; chorale melody by Bach

Nachspiel: *Das alte Jahr vergangen ist* (The old year has passed) Steuerlein; Bach chorale

Acknowledgements

For editorial advice grateful thanks must be given to Pamela Smith; Martin Holmes, Alfred Brendel Curator of Music, Bodleian Library; Colin Homiski, Research Librarian, Music, Senate House Library; R. Larry Todd, Arts and Sciences Distinguished Professor of Music, Duke University, North Carolina. Further editorial advice was received from Prof. Susan Wollenberg, Dr Caroline Potter, Jeremy Polmear, Stephen Carpenter, Stephen Johnson, Christopher Hum and James Rose.

Epigram translations are by Professor Marian Wilson Kimber, University of Iowa, College of Liberal Arts and Sciences, School of Music. The translation of Uhland's *Im Herbste* on p. 78 and p. 125 is by Sharon Krebs.

Thanks are also due to the publishers for their permission to reprint the letters from Marcia J. Citron (trans. and ed.), *The Letters of Fanny Hensel to Felix Mendelssohn* (New York: Pendragon Press, 1987), and Rudolf Elvers and Craig Tomlinson (eds), *Mendelssohn, A Life in Letters* (London: Cassell/Orion Publishing Group, 1986).

Picture credits

Bibliography

Citron, Marcia (trans. and ed.), *The Letters of Fanny Hensel to Felix Mendelssohn* (New York: Pendragon Press, 1987)

Devrient, Eduard, *Meine Erinnerungen an Felix Mendelssohn-Bartholdy* (Leipzig: J. J. Weber, 1869)

Elvers, Rudolf and Craig Tomlinson, *Felix Mendelssohn, A Life in Letters* (London: Cassell, 1986)

Hensel, Sebastian, *The Mendelssohn Family (1729–1847) From Letters & Journals*, 2 vols (New York: Harper & Brothers, 1882)

Marx, Adolf Bernhard, *Erinnerungen aus meinem Leben* (Berlin: Otto Janke, 1865)

Mendelssohn-Bartholdy, Karl, *Goethe and Mendelssohn (1821–1831)* (London: Macmillan & Co, 1872)

Moscheles, Charlotte, *Life of Moscheles, with Selections from his Diaries and Correspondence* (Hansebooks, 2019)

Nichols, Roger, *Mendelssohn Remembered* (London: Faber & Faber, 1997)

Radcliffe, Philip, *Mendelssohn* (The Master Musicians, London: Dent, 1954/1990)

Reynolds, Christopher Alan, *Motives for Allusion: Context and Content in Nineteenth-Century Music* (Cambridge, Mass: Harvard Press, 2003)

Todd, R. Larry, *Mendelssohn: A Life in Music* (Oxford: Oxford University Press, 2003)

——, *Fanny Hensel, The Other Mendelssohn* (Oxford: Oxford University Press, 2010)

Tillard, Françoise, *Fanny Mendelssohn* (Portland: Amadeus Press, 1992)

Wilson Kimber, Marian, 'Fanny Hensel's Seasons of Life: Poetic Epigrams, Vignettes, and Meaning', *Journal of Musicological Research*, October 2008

Recommended recordings

Scottish Symphony: Chamber Orchestra of Europe/Yannick Nézét-Seguin: DG 4797337.
  Hungarian State Orchestra/Ivan Fischer: Hungaroton HCD 12660-2
Das Jahr: YouTube: Jessica Wei Zhu; (or Lauma Skride: Sony 88697 03016-2)
  Els Biesemans, Fortepiano, *Das Jahr* by Mendelssohn-Hensel, Genuin 12244 (2012)

Notes

1. The Mendelssohns and Enlightenment Berlin

1 Letter of 18 June 1825, in Karl Mendelssohn-Bartholdy, *Goethe and Mendelssohn (1821–1831)* (London: Macmillan & Co, 1872), p. 55
2 Michael P. Steinberg, 'Culture, Gender and Music: A Forum on the Mendelssohn Family', *Musical Quarterly*, vol. 77, issue 4, 1993, p. 648
3 Shakespeare, *A Midsummer Night's Dream*, Act 3 Scene 2
4 Adolf Bernhard Marx, *Erinnerungen aus meinem Leben* (Berlin: Otto Janke, 1865), pp. 110–17
5 Eduard Devrient, *Meine Erinnerungen an Felix Mendelssohn-Bartholdy* (Leipzig: J. J. Weber, 1869), pp. 8–9
6 Felix Mendelssohn, 9 December 1835, *Sämtliche Briefe in 12 Bänden*, eds Juliette Appold and Regina Back (Kassel: Bärenreiter, 2008), ii, p. 106

2. Felix

1 George R. Marek, *Gentle Genius: The Story of Felix Mendelssohn* (London: Hale, 1973), p. 91
2 Charles Edward Horsley, 'Reminiscences of Mendelssohn'. First published in *Dwight's Journal of Music* (Boston), and reprinted in *The Choir* (London) for 11 and 25 January, and 8 and 15 February 1873 respectively
3 *The Soldier's Love*, libretto by Johann Ludwig Caspar, premiered on Felix's twelfth birthday
4 Sebastian Hensel, *The Mendelssohn Family (1729–1847) From Letters & Journals*, 2 vols (New York: Harper & Brothers, 1882), p. 135
5 Roger Nichols, *Mendelssohn Remembered* (London: Faber & Faber, 1997), p. 10
6 Quoted in Melvin Berger, *Guide to Chamber Music* (Dover Publications, 2001), p. 266
7 Nichols, *Mendelssohn Remembered*, p. 11
8 R. Larry Todd, *Mendelssohn: A Life in Music* (Oxford: Oxford University Press, 2003), p. 194
9 'Felix Mendelssohn: Reviving the Works of J. S. Bach', Library of Congress webpage: https://www.loc.gov/item/ihas.200156436/
10 André Pirro, *J. S. Bach*, trans. by Mervyn Savill (New York: Orion Press, 1957)
11 Felix's letter to Marc-André Souchay, 15 October 1842, from *Selected Letters of Mendelssohn*, ed. W. F. Alexander (London: Swan Sonnenschein & Co., 1894), p. 124
12 Hensel, *The Mendelssohn Family*, i, p. 91
13 R. Larry Todd, *Fanny Hensel* (Oxford: Oxford University Press, 2010), p. 105

3. The Grand Tour and Felix's Scottish Journey

1   Johann Wolfgang von Goethe, *Italian Journey* (Harmondsworth: Penguin, 1970), p. 13

2   Ibid., p. 128

3   Ibid., p. 147

4   Hensel, *The Mendelssohn Family*, i, p. 123

5   Letter of Mendelssohn to Klingemann, 15 April 1846, Bodleian Library, Oxford, MS. M.D.M. d.40, ff. 312–13

6   George Grove (ed.), *A Dictionary of Music and Musicians* (London: Macmillan & Co., 1900), p. 262

7   Friedrich Silcher wrote to Schumann in 1837 saying that all Beethoven's music sounded Ossianic

8   Hyperion Records, *Ossian's Lied nach dem Falle Nathos*, D278: https://www.hyperion-records.co.uk/tw.asp?w=W2028

9   Stuart Kelly, *Scott-land: The Man who Invented a Nation* (Edinburgh: Polygon, 2011)

10 David Jenkins and Mark Visocchi, *Mendelssohn in Scotland* (London: Chappell & Co, 1978), p. 58

11 Hans Günter Klein and Rudolf Elvers (eds), *Fanny Hensel: Tagebücher* (Leipzig: Breitkopf & Härtel, 2002)

12 Felix Mendelssohn, *Sämtliche Briefe in 12 Bänden*, Appold and Back (eds), i, p. 265

13 Charlotte Moscheles, *Life of Moscheles* (London: Hurst and Blackett, 1873), i, pp. 99–100

14 The Victorian Web, *Felix Mendelssohn and the Nineteenth-Century Musical Scene in Victorian England*, http://victorianweb.org/mt/mendelssohn/savant2.html

15 Quoted in Philip Radcliffe, *Mendelssohn* (London: Dent, 1954), p. 29

16 Nichols, *Mendelssohn Remembered*, p. 61

17 Klingemann letter, 7 December 1827, in Hensel, *The Mendelssohn Family*, i, p. 146

18 Jenkins and Visocchi, *Mendelssohn in Scotland*, pp. 40–1

19 Rudolf Elvers and Craig Tomlinson (eds), *Felix Mendelssohn: A Life in Letters* (London: Cassell, 1986), p. 81. He refers to Bad Doberan, a resort situated near the Baltic Sea, where sea swimming was recognised as beneficial to health

20 Letter to his father, 28 July 1829, Edinburgh, in Hensel, *The Mendelssohn Family*, i, p. 196

21 History of Albany Street, Edinburgh: https://sites.google.com/site/albanystreet edinburgh/further-backround/musicians

22 Elvers and Tomlinson, *Felix Mendelssohn: A Life in Letters*, p. 89

23 Mendelssohn letter, 30 July 1829, in Hensel, *The Mendelssohn Family*, i, p. 198

24 Letter from Edinburgh, 28 July 1829, in Hensel, *The Mendelssohn Family*, i, p. 197

25 Elvers and Tomlinson, *Felix Mendelssohn: A Life in Letters*, p. 85

26 'Mendelssohn in Scotland, Tummel Bridge' webpage: https://www.mendelssohninscotland.com/highlands-tummel-bridge-fort-william

27 Hensel, *The Mendelssohn Family*, i, pp. 202–3

28 Elvers and Tomlinson, *Felix Mendelssohn: A Life in Letters*, p. 90

29 Letter from Mull, 26 July 1818, in *Life, Letters and Literary Remains of John Keats* (London: Edward Moxon, 1848), p. 185

30 Letter to Abraham, 7 August 1829, in Elvers and Tomlinson, *Felix Mendelssohn: A Life in Letters*, pp. 87–8

31 Jenkins and Visocchi, *Mendelssohn in Scotland*, p. 73

32 Fanny was recently pregnant with her son. Sebastian was born on 16 June 1830

33 Marcia J. Citron (ed.), *The Letters of Fanny Hensel to Felix Mendelssohn* (New York: Pendragon Press, 1987), p. 73

4. The *Hebrides Overture*

1   Letter, 7 August 1829, in Elvers and Tomlinson, *Felix Mendelssohn: A Life in Letters*, p. 87

2   *Letters of Felix Mendelssohn-Bartholdy from Italy and Switzerland*, trans. Lady Wallace (London: Longman, Roberts & Green, 1864), p. 332

3   Todd, *Mendelssohn*, p. 260

4   Elvers and Tomlinson, *Felix Mendelssohn: A Life in Letters*, p. 130

5   David Cairns (trans. and ed.), *The Memoirs of Hector Berlioz* (Everyman Library Classics, 2002), p. 659

6   Edward Lockspeiser, *Music and Painting: A Study in Comparative Ideas from Turner to Schoenberg* (London: Cassell, 1973)

7   Myles Birket Foster, *History of the Philharmonic Society of London 1813–1912* (London: John Lane, 1912), p. 214

8   Elvers and Tomlinson, *Felix Mendelssohn: A Life in Letters*, p. 184

9   Douglas Seaton comment, in the *Cambridge Companion to Mendelssohn* (Cambridge: Cambridge University Press, 2004)

10 R. Larry Todd, *Mendelssohn: The Hebrides and Other Overtures* (Cambridge: Cambridge University Press, 1993), p. 35

11 Classic FM, Mendelssohn: https://www.classicfm.com/composers/mendelssohn/guides/felix-mendelssohn-musical-style

12 George Hamilton, 'Melodies entwined – the love story of Felix Mendelssohn', *Independent.ie*, 28 March 2020: https://www.independent.ie/entertainment/music/melodies-entwined-the-love-story-of-felix-mendelssohn-39079635.html

13 Radcliffe, *Mendelssohn*, p. 31

14 Shakespeare, *Coriolanus*, Act 2 Scene 1; Coriolanus addressing his wife, Volumnia

5. The *Scottish Symphony*

1   Elvers & Tomlinson, *Felix Mendelssohn: A Life in Letters*, p. 144

2   Todd, *Mendelssohn*, p. 434

3   Ibid., p. 438

4   BIS CD booklet: https://www.eclassical.com/shop/art19/BIS-SACD-1604_booklet pdf-1088aa.pdf

5   Rey M. Longyear, 'Cyclic Form and Tonal Relationships in Mendelssohn's *Scottish Symphony*', *Musical Quarterly* 56, 1970

6   Charles Gounod, *Autobiographical Reminiscences* (London: Heineman, 1896), pp. 123–4

7   Mendelssohn in Scotland, Loch Lomond: https://mendelssohninscotland.com/glasgow-loch-lomond-and-trossachs

8   Wilfred Blunt, *On Wings of Song: A Biography of Felix Mendelssohn* (London: Hamilton, 1974), p. 129

9   Citron (ed.), *Letters of Fanny Hensel to Felix Mendelssohn*, p. 151

10 Fanny's letter to Rebecka, 5 December 1843, in Hensel, *The Mendelssohn Family*, ii, p. 236

11 Hensel, *The Mendelssohn Family*, i, pp. 284–5

12 Sir Julius Benedict, *Sketch of the Life and Works of the late Felix Mendelssohn* (London: John Murray, 1850), pp. 24–5

13 As a rough guide, a craftsman earned about 200 thaler a year

14 Nichols, *Mendelssohn Remembered*, pp. 138–9

15 Harold C. Schonberg, *The Great Pianists* (London: Gollancz, 1965), p. 218

16 Hensel, *The Mendelssohn Family*, ii, p. 276

17 Hensel, *The Mendelssohn Family*, ii, p. 292

18 F. G. Edwards, *The History of Mendelssohn's Oratorio 'Elijah'*, (London: Novello, 1896), p. 86

19 Classic fm, Mendelssohn, 'Music in Nature': https://www.classicfm.com/composers/mendelssohn/guides/scotland-holyrood/nature-sketch/

20 Lawyer; from 1834 on the Board of the Leipzig Gewandhaus

21 The Schuncks were the family of Cécile's sister

22 Joseph Joachim, violin virtuoso from Hungary

23 Moscheles, *Life of Moscheles*, ii, p. 169–70

24 Nichols, *Mendelssohn Remembered*, p. 238

25 Birket Foster, *History of the Philharmonic Society*, p. 199

6. Fanny

1 Hensel, *The Mendelssohn Family*, i, p. 73

2 Ibid., ii, p. 31

3 George R. Marek, *Gentle Genius: The Story of Felix Mendelssohn* (New York: Funk & Wagnalls, 1972)

4 Hensel, *The Mendelssohn Family*, i, pp. 88–9

5 David Conway, *Jewry in Music: Entry to the Profession from the Enlightenment to Richard Wagner* (Cambridge: Cambridge University Press, 2012)

6 Todd, *Fanny Hensel*, p. 146

7 Hensel, *The Mendelssohn Family*, i, p. 82

8 'Proposal to Establish an Instrumental Lovers' Association', bound with Fanny's diaries in MA Depos. Berlin 500, 22

9 Todd, *Fanny Hensel*, p. 119

10 Citron (ed.), *Letters of Fanny Hensel to Felix Mendelssohn*, p. 91

11 They had playful readings from the novelist Jean Paul Richter in the house

12 Marcia J. Citron 'The Lieder of Fanny Mendelssohn Hensel', *Musical Quarterly* 49 (1983), p. 571

13 Sheila Hayman, 'A Fanny Mendelssohn Masterpiece Finally Gets Its Due', *Guardian*, 8 March 2017

14 A poem by Heinrich Heine, set to music by Felix in 1834, Op. 34 No. 2

15 1 February 1847, in Citron (ed.), *Letters of Fanny Hensel to Felix Mendelssohn*, p. 363

16 Todd, *Fanny Hensel*, p. 89

17 Hensel, *The Mendelssohn Family*, i, p. 84

18 Todd, *Fanny Hensel*, p. 123

19 Klein and Elvers (eds), *Fanny Hensel: Tagebücher*, p. 104

20 Staatsbibliothek zu Berlin, Mendelssohn Archive, MS 158

21 Todd, *Fanny Hensel*, p. 225

22 Details in Hans-Günter Klein, *Fanny Hensels öffentliche Auftritte als Pianistin*, MS 14, 2005a, pp. 287–8

23 Fanny's letter to Klingemann, 15 February 1838, in Hensel, *The Mendelssohn Family*, ii, p. 37

24 Hensel, *The Mendelssohn Family*, i, p. 229

25 Fanny's letter to Felix, 22 November 1836, in Citron (ed.), *Letters of Fanny Hensel to Felix Mendelssohn*, p. 222

26 Hensel, *The Mendelssohn Family*, various accounts of the Sunday gatherings

27 Felix to Fanny, 24 January 1837, in Hensel, *The Mendelssohn Family*, ii, p. 31

7. The Italian Journey

1 Encyclopaedia Britannica, Goethe *Italian Journey*: https://www.britannica.com/biography/Johann-Wolfgang-von-Goethe/Italian-journey-1786-88
2 Goethe, *Italian Journey*, p. 413
3 Ibid., pp. 483, 490
4 Hensel, *The Mendelssohn Family*, ii, p. 57
5 Hensel, *The Mendelssohn Family*, ii, p. 63
6 *Letters of Felix Mendelssohn-Bartholdy from Italy and Switzerland*, p. 101
7 Hensel, *The Mendelssohn Family*, ii, p. 66
8 Ibid., p. 67
9 In Rome's old coinage 60 *paoli* (*guili*) = 20 *testone* = 6 *scudi*; twenty artichokes, or a theatre ticket, cost 1 *guili*
10 Citron (ed.), *Letters of Fanny Hensel to Felix Mendelssohn*, p. 286
11 Hensel, *The Mendelssohn Family*, ii, p. 75
12 This quote has caused confusion, as none of Felix's *Songs without Words* were ever thought to be by Fanny
13 Hensel, *The Mendelssohn Family*, ii, p. 101
14 Todd, *Fanny Hensel*, pp. 242–3
15 Citron (ed.), *Letters of Fanny Hensel to Felix Mendelssohn*, p. 282
16 Gounod, *Autobiographical Reminiscences*, p. 91
17 Goethe, *Italian Journey*, p. 447
18 Ibid., pp. 447–56
19 Ibid., p. 470
20 Hensel, *The Mendelssohn Family*, ii, p. 86
21 Ibid., p. 88
22 Ibid., p. 93
23 Ibid., p. 101
24 Ibid., p. 96
25 Owned by a Russian princess and used as an artistic salon; now it is the official residence of the British ambassador to Italy in Rome
26 Hensel, *The Mendelssohn Family*, ii, p. 118
27 Ibid., p. 112
28 Ibid., p. 121
29 On the coast, about fifty-six kilometres south-east of Rome
30 Probably coined earlier in the nineteenth century, meaning, it's so beautiful, one can die peacefully after seeing Naples
31 Goethe, *Italian Journey*, p. 215
32 Hensel, *The Mendelssohn Family*, ii, p. 144
33 Hensel, *The Mendelssohn Family*, ii, p. 157

8. *Das Jahr*

1 Hensel, *The Mendelssohn Family*, ii, p. 103
2 *Journal of Musicological Research* 27 (2008), pp. 359–95
3 H. C. Robbins Landon, *Haydn: Chronicle and Works* (London: Thames & Hudson, 1976–80), v, p. 120
4 Citron (ed.), *Letters of Fanny Hensel to Felix Mendelssohn*, pp. 483, 485, 548
5 Simon likened winter to old age; this in turn quoted Mozart's Symphony K550; Robbins Landon, *Haydn: Chronicle and Works, 1801–1809* (London: Thames & Hudson, 1994), p. 180
6 Quoted in Hans-Günther Klein, *Jahrbuch Preussischer Kulturbesitz* 35, 1999, p. 271
7 Klein and Elvers (eds), *Fanny Hensel: Tagebücher*, pp. 270–1

8 In artworks, the psaltery is sometimes seen among the muses

9 Christopher Alan Reynolds, *Motives for Allusion: Context and Content in Nineteenth-Century Music* (Cambridge, Mass: Harvard Press, 2003)

10 Nos 29 and 30: *Jesus it is finished*

11 Johann Ludwig Uhland, 'Frühlingsglaube' from *Frühlingslieder*, No. 2, in *Werke*, i, *Gedichte, Dramen, Versepik und Prosa* (Frankfurt: Insel, 1983), pp 44–5

12 In Goethe's *Trilogy of Passion, Werther, II Elegy*

13 Bach also wrote a chorale prelude on the theme, BWV 614, included in his *Orgelbüchlein* (1712–13)

14 Moris Senegor, 'Schumann, Carnaval (1835)', Insight Lecture for Stockton Symphony, California: https://www.morissenegor.com/musical-conversations/schumann-carnaval-1835/

15 Christian Thorau, *Vom Klang zur Metapher: Perspektiven der musikalischen Analyse* (Hildesheim: Georg Olms, 2012)

16 *The Life of William Sterndale Bennett* (Cambridge, 1907), pp 126–7

17 Hensel, *The Mendelssohn Family*, ii, p. 260

18 Ibid., p. 257

19 Ibid., p. 324

20 Ibid., p. 325

21 Citron (ed.), *Letters of Fanny Hensel to Felix Mendelssohn*, p. 349

22 Todd, *Fanny Hensel*, p. 315

23 Ibid., p. 316

24 Fanny Hensel, *Das Jahr. Ein Klavierzyklus. Faksimile* (Furore Verlag, 2000)

25 Klein and Elvers (eds), *Fanny Hensel: Tagebücher*, pp. 264–6

26 Hensel, *The Mendelssohn Family*, ii, p. 334

27 James Keller, *Chamber Music: A Listener's Guide* (London: Oxford University Press, 2014), p. 249

9. Legacies

1 Todd, *Fanny Hensel*, p. 288

2 S. Schmidler, et al., 'Felix Mendelssohn: the mystery of his early death', *Fortschritte der Neurologie-Psychologie*, September 2006, pp. 522–7

3 Hensel, *The Mendelssohn Family*, ii, p. 337

4 Sleeve notes to the *Quatuor Ébène* Erato recording of Felix and Fanny Mendelssohn String Quartets

5 Hensel, *The Family Mendelssohn*, ii, p. 335

6 Ibid.

7 Wilhelm Adolf Lampadius, *The Life of Felix Mendelssohn-Bartholdy* (Boston: Oliver Sitson, 1887), p.163

8 Georg Knepler, *Musikgeschichte des 19 Jahrhunderts* (Berlin: Henschelverlag, 1961), ii, p. 770

9 'Jenny Lind at Exeter-Hall', *The Times*, 11 December 1855

10 L. G. D. Sanders, 'Jenny Lind, Sullivan and the Mendelssohn Scholarship', *Musical Times*, 1956

11 Clara Schumann, quoted in George Grove (ed.), *A Dictionary of Music and Musicians* (London: Macmillan, 1880), p. 298

12 *Cambridge Companion to Mendelssohn* (Cambridge: Cambridge University Press, 2004)

13 Robert R. Reilly, 'Mendelssohn – Great or Also-Ran?', *Crisis* 16, No. 9, October 1998, pp. 49–51

14 Felix Mendelssohn, *Sämtliche Briefe in 12 Bänden*, eds Juliette Appold and Regina Back (Kassel: Bärenreiter, 2008)

15 'Felix Mendelssohn: His Music and Legacy', on Compositional Endeavour webpage: https://compositionalendeavor.wordpress.com/2010/06/11/felix-mendelssohn-his-music-and-legacy/

16 Grove Music online: *Mendelssohn, Felix*, section 14, *Reception*

17 Renate Hellwig-Unruh, *Fanny Hensel geb. Mendelssohn Bartholdy: thematisches Verzeichnis der Kompositionen*, (Adliswil: Kunzelmann, 2000)

18 Klein and Elvers (eds), *Fanny Hensel: Tagebücher*, pp. 277–9

19 From *Allgemeine musikalische Zeiting*, 1847, quoted in Stephen Rodgers, 'Fanny Hensel's Schematic Fantasies; or The Art of Beginning', in Laurel Parsons and Brenda Ravenscroft (eds), *Analytical Essays on Music by Women Composers* (Oxford: Oxford University Press, 2008), p. 151

20 Todd, *Fanny Hensel*, p. 346

21 Text by Joseph Freiherr von Eichendorff; the song was released posthumously as Op. 10 No. 5

The Letters

1   Johann Gustav Droysen, academic and historian who taught Felix, and was described by Fanny thus: 'A nineteen-year-old philologist imbued with all the freshness and lively, active sympathy typical of his age, with knowledge beyond his years and a pure poetic sensibility and healthy kind nature'

2   He refers to the *Gartenhaus*, at the family home, Leipziger Strasse 3, in Berlin

3   Isola Bella is an island on Lake Maggiore

4   Villa Pisani, from *c.*1555, a grand villa in the Veneto region

5   Possibly referring to the lute in *The Pastoral Concert*, by the Renaissance Venetian, now in the Musée du Louvre

6   *The Entombment of Christ*, *c.*1522, also in the Louvre

7   Altarpiece panel painting (1515–18) by Titian, in the position it was painted for in the Santa Maria Gloriosa dei Frari Church, Venice

8   Meaning: stand two ancient Greek lions

9   Meaning: braggart

10 From 1497, possibly a collaborative effort with Mariotto Albertinelli, now in the cathedral at Volterra

11 In the heart of the city, *Villetta di Negro* has a scenic panorama, created in the late nineteenth century

12 Aleatico is a variety of Italian red wine grape

13 The bibliophile Fortunato Santini, who had praised Felix in 1830

14 The singing refers to Tamino's aria in Mozart's opera *The Magic Flute*

15 Wilhelm Hensel had visited Italy previously in 1825–8

16 August Grahl was another artist friend of Hensel's, and had visited Rome with him

17 Ludwig Landsberg, German violinist, formerly of the Berlin *Königsstädtisches Theater*, then in Rome

18 Johann Daniel Kestner, doll-maker, from Thuringia, Germany

19 Shepherds from the Volsker mountains, who were pipers, came to Rome in the Advent period

20 'Your brother who plays the cello so well' – Paul

21 Italian painter and engraver, Luigi Calamatta

22 Hensel's connections from his previous Italian visit eased the couple's way, including visiting the papal apartments

23 Rooms, including the Heliodorus (Gift of the Sun) room in the Vatican, used for private audiences

24 A painting from 1514, by Raphael, depicting a 1263 miracle episode in Bolsena

25 Meaning 'English soup' – an Italian dessert of custard and sponge cake

26 Ferdinand Hiller was a composer, conductor and pianist, and a family friend
27 *The Destruction of Jerusalem*, Op. 42; the oratorio was premiered at the Leipzig Gewandhaus, 2 April 1840
28 Marie Pleyel, Belgian concert pianist
29 Prussian major general who served as adjutant to the younger brother of Frederick William III
30 E.g. in paintings by Jean-Léon Gérôme, and from 1827 by Sir David Wilkie
31 Part of an ancient noble Roman family
32 Ceiling fresco by Guido Reni for the Casino (garden house) adjacent to the Palazzo Pallavicini-Rospigliosi
33 Prince Leopold of the Two Sicilies (1813–60)
34 Fat Thursday, which marks the start of the celebrations
35 The painter August Kaselowsky was a pupil of Hensel's, and made a sketch of Fanny
36 Candles
37 Walkways
38 Painted in 1515, now in the Uffizi Gallery in Florence
39 The use of 'parallel fifths' in music was considered forbidden, sounding like a loss of independence in the part-writing
40 The Congregation Sisters of the Most Holy Trinity, founded in 1762
41 Northern wind
42 'I've been killed'
43 Luigi Lablache, Italian bass singer
44 Felix's Psalm 95, Op. 46, *Come let us sing*, for choir and orchestra
45 The Battle of Nezib between Egypt and the Ottoman Empire took place in 1839
46 Karl Wolfgang Paul Mendelssohn-Bartholdy, Felix and Cécile's eldest son (1838–97)
47 Julie Schunk (1816–75) was Cécile Jeanrenaud's sister; she married Julius Schunck in 1839. Felix played the organ at their wedding; some believe this was the first performance of his 'Wedding March'
48 Otto von Worringen was president of the Prussian government of the Rhineland province, in Düsseldorf; a supporter and close friend of Felix
49 Their sister, Rebecka, was pregnant with Ernst Gustav Paul Dirichlet, who was born 9 November 1840
50 About thirty kilometres south-east of Naples, on the Bay of Naples
51 Villa Medici, where the Prix de Rome winners stayed
52 Bach, spoken with a French accent
53 Fortunato Santini, Italian priest in Rome and patron of music, whom Felix visited in 1830
54 Fanny had written her *Oratorium nach Bildern der Bibel* in 1831; it is also known as her *Cholera Cantata*
55 Liszt made nine transcriptions for solo piano of the Beethoven symphonies; the first series was dedicated to Ingres
56 Gaspare Spontini, Italian opera composer
57 She refers to a painting by Goya of the Spanish Inquisition (1812–19)
58 Cécile was pregnant with their third child
59 Felix befriended the Alexander family in 1829; it included Sir Alexander and three daughters
60 In 1840 the remains of Napoleon (who died nearly two decades earlier) were returned to France for burial from the island of St Helena
61 In the Alban Hills, some thirty kilometres from Rome
62 Pauline Garcia was a leading French mezzo-soprano, teacher and composer
63 Wilhelmine Schröder-Devrient, a popular operatic soprano
64 Beethoven song, Op. 46, composed 1795–6
65 Felix refers to his Psalm 114, Op. 51, *Da Israel aus Aegypten zog*
66 Eduard Grell, a German composer, organist and music teacher

Index